Passy Amaraegbu

BREAK

THAT

STUBBORN

HABIT

i

BREAK THAT STUBBORN HABIT

e-mail-drpassy@yahoo.com

ISBN: 978-978-958-755-1

Published by
Wisdom Literary & Management Agency,
wisdomliterary@gmail.com

Graphic Concept + Design: Victor Olukoju

+234(0)808 040 8977 (Nigeria)
www.victorolukoju.org
fourthmancreation@yahoo.com
info@victorolukoju.org

No. 12 Irepodun Street,
Akiode Bus Stop, Ojodu, Lagos State.

Except otherwise stated all scriptural quotations are from the New King James Version (NKJV) of the Holy Bible.

BREAK THAT STUBBORN HABIT

Commendation for Break That Stubborn Habit

Dr. Passy in his characteristic manner has dropped in the hands of many individuals who are sincerely battling self-destructive and humiliating habits a very practical escape route in this text. I am sure that both these persons and those that seeks to help them will find this book a useful working manual. This generation will remain grateful to Dr. Passy for a wonderful work.

Prof. Benjamin Ndukwu
University of Port Harcourt
Rivers State, Nigeria.

The book is written in a very simple language with introductory story and illustrations to drive home the content of each chapter. The book does not just bring up actions that could help break up stubborn habits, but also provides guide to appropriate habits. It is a book reference for academic reading for people involved in counselling, behavior modification, and other attitude change programme. It is as well good for religious enthusiasts.

Benjamin O. Ehigie, Ph.D
Professor & Head
Department of Psychology, University of Ibadan.

"Breaking that stubborn habit", by Dr. Passy Amaraegbu, is a timely book for a generation where many are overwhelmed with stubborn habits and have given up trying to break them. In today's world, these habits have festered due to several factors including peer pressures, changing (including foreign) cultures, and technology (especially the Internet and social media)

Dr. Passy Amaraegbu, clearly draws on his doctoral qualifications in psychology ad theology to present the secular and spiritual dimensions of the challenge, and this is evident throughout the book. The book is written in an essay to read style, and each chapter is structured with anecdotal evidence, detailed analysis and a useful summary. In my opinion, more weight should have been given to the sections on breaking the habits – e.g. by including "how to" steps, recommendations (to do or avoid) for common habits to be broken and testimonies of those who have overcome stubborn habits. I therefore think a follow-up book is an urgent necessity.

Overall, this is a very insightful book on the scourge of bad, stubborn habits and the challenge of overcoming them. It is recommended for counsellors, parents and those seeking to overcome stubborn habits.

Bar. Nickolas Nyamali
Group Chairman
Investment One.

NB: In response to Barrister Nick's request, I have included the issues he raised in the last two chapters (11 and 12) of the book.

This book **Break That Stubborn Habit** is highly recommended as a "must read" for everyone, because habits are so significant in the lives of people that they stand as signposts which announce our personalities and consequently every noble effort geared towards obtaining freedom from stubborn habits is worthwhile, as consequences of engaging in stubborn habits surpass the benefits. This book is an operational manual that helps people in understanding stubborn habits, development of stubborn habits, the issues which promote stubborn habits in the lives of people, consequences of indulging in stubborn habits, principles of breaking stubborn habits as well as victory stories over stubborn habits. This book will help you kick-start a revolution of regaining your personal freedom from stubborn habits and to break the chains of recidivism, while the resources wasted in the satisfaction of stubborn habits can be reinvested in the pursuit of noble lifestyle and a new foundation laid for successful living.

*Dave **Inyere***
Former Manager, Business Optimization and Process Improvement, Chevron, Nigeria.

Tables/Diagrammes

Page

Dedication

To,

Every soul who is sincerely fighting to win the war
against stubborn habits.

May you go from struggle to survival,
From survival to success,
Finally, from success to significance.

Acknowledgement

I use this opportunity to appreciate Felix Ogharandukun Chibuzor Osazee and my first son, Nwachukwu Chinonye for their painstaking editorial efforts. My thanks go to Pastor David Okodua for sharing his intellectual expertise which was helpful in the publication of this book.

For over a decade, Kemi Matthew has rendered invaluable computer services to my personal and corporate ministries. God bless her abundantly. In the same manner, I appreciate our other office staff namely, Pastor Ignatius Ihejirika, the Administrator, Ikechukwu Timothy, the accountant, Paulinus Ngumah, Julius Nwachukwu and Tony Samuel for their diverse assistance in the course of writing this book.

My appreciation goes to Nick Nyamali, Dave Inyere, Dave Michael and Mike Akpan for their supports toward publishing the book. In the same vein, I thank Professors, Ben Ehigie and Ben Ndukwu for their commendation. My special thanks goes to Dr. Cosmas Ilechukwu for writing the foreword.

Finally I use this opportunity to appreciate my wife and children for their continued support and prayers for me. God bless you all abundantly.

Passy Amaraegbu Ph.D, DMin.
Grace Palace,
Surulere, Lagos, Nigeria
January 2017

Author's Preface

Habit, the subject matter of this book is an issue that has universal relevance and application. Everywhere human beings exist, they display their habits. These habits turn around to determine people's self-worth (personal view of self) and self esteem (others view of self).

This book, focuses on the crucial issue of how to handle difficult negative habits. These habits are troublesome, and tiring to mortals. They frustrate personal purpose and progress. They serve as excess luggages and stumbling blocks on people's way to success.

Consequently, multitudes of people are caught in this web of personal and prolonged struggle against stubborn habits. Without regard to age or affiliation, complexion or creed, social or spiritual status, human beings are at different stages in their war against various stubborn habits.

Writing from the vantage position of a professional, as well as a deep wealth of experience, the author presents a classic material. *Break that Stubborn Habit* will challenge and change your life, instruct and inspire you to be the best you were created to be. In this twelve relevant and potent chapters of the book, the reader will find satisfaction and strength, hope and healing.

Foreword

"Old habits die hard," declared Jocelyn Murray, in her grippingly fascinating historical fiction, *The Roman General: A Novel.* Habits are automatic behaviours which one develops overtime through conscious repetitions until they become unconscious patterns of behaviour and form part of one's personality. Humans are animals of habits, because we can hardly function properly without them. We live by a rhythm of involuntary actions which has become routine behaviours. The first few times we carry out an action, it is usually a very conscious and deliberate response to a conscious decision. Repeating the same action several times will make it to become hard-coded into our subconscious mind and thus becomes a habit. Habit defines our character which in turn determines our personality. Habits are functionally relevant to us in mind management. Things we do habitually no longer encumber our conscious mind but free it to pay attention to fewer things. However, not every habit is good. A good habit is a pattern of consistent behaviour that is beneficial to one's spiritual, mental and physical wellbeing. A daily routine of bible reading and prayer are good examples of a good habit. Regular exercise, eating balanced diet and at the right time, reading good books etc are all good habits.

Some habits are bad and very destructive in their effects. Bad habits belong to the category of destructive behaviour more commonly known as addictions. In this book, *Break That Stubborn Habit*, the author calls our attention to some of the very bad habits that wield very addictive influence over their victims and shows us how to deal with them. He mentioned among several others such bad and stubborn habits as drug addiction, smoking, late-coming and absenteeism, alcoholism, pilfering, lying and sexual promiscuity. He lamented that "the long term consequences of these shameful habits is a life of mediocrity and misery." Besides, Dr Amaraegbu cited real life stories, to buttress the point that stubborn habits had led to the downfall of many and to the early death of some others. Very obvious in the thesis of this book is the complicity of the devil in hatching, nurturing and sustaining stubborn habits. This fuelled the author's conviction that wilful continuance in these habits can lead to eternal doom.

Being a clinical psychologist by training and a consummate pastor by vocation, the author drawing from a rich intellectual know-how of a practitioner, and the compassionate heart of a pastor, bemoans stubborn habits as "an unnecessary burden to bear, a wasteful lifestyle to maintain, and an unprofitable business to engage in." He recommends a combination of psychological therapy and divine intervention through prayers/deliverance as the best way to gain lasting freedom from the strangleholds of stubborn habits. Owning up one's stubborn habit and being open to discuss it with competent professionals is the first major step to breaking them. If you need to take this first major step, do please take it now.

Perusing the manuscript of this book elicited a loud WOW from me. This is a book that demands close study. It is a very veritable resource for lecturers and students of psychology, for pastors, deliverance ministers, and indeed every christian who is dealing with some stubborn habits. *Break That Stubborn Habit* is not only informative; it is intellectually challenging and spiritually refreshing. Get it and enjoy it.

Cosmas Ilechukwu *DMin.*
General Overseer,
Charismatic Renewal Ministries (CRM) Inc.
Chairman of the Global Governing Council of
International Ministers Forum (IMF)

The life Span of Stubborn Habits

S/N	STAGE	FEATURES
1.	Sowing	a. Onset of Stubborn Habit b. Level of conditioning depends on the potency of content. c. Short memory
2.	Seedling	a. Fast growth or death of habit. b. Strong battle for existence. c. Exertion of pressure to survive
3.	Maturity	a. Consolidation b. Establishment of pattern. c. Access to three levels of memory. (Short, mid and long term) d. Beginning of stigmatization
4.	Fruiting	a. Massive productive activities. b. Multiplication of similar habits. c. Complexity in nature. d. Establishment of stigmatization. e. Domination of all levels of memory.
5.	Decline	a. Weakness of the habit b. Development of guilt c. Inner cry for help d. Consequences reach Zenith degree.

NB: Victory over stubborn habit can occur at any of these stages. However, the earlier it occurs, the better and easier.

Chapter One

UNDERSTANDING STUBBORN HABITS

He was in his mid-thirties; a Master's degree holder and former lecturer in an American University who lost a promising career and family to drug addiction. I met him during a Group therapy session in a psychiatric hospital. The horrible consequences of his foolish habit led to his deportation to Nigeria and he ended up in a psychiatric hospital. This was in 1988 while I was engaged in compulsory internship as part of my training as a clinical psychologist. It was a very pitiable situation. A case of paradise lost.

The essence of this story is in relation to formation of habits. The former Nigerian-born American don learnt to depend on drugs and they ruined his life.

What then is a habit? A habit is "an action one performs often and almost without thinking; a usual way of doing something; an addiction".[1] Another definition is that a habit is:

> a pattern of behaviour or established practice or custom. In learning theory, habit is a learned behavioural response associated with a particular situation,

---

[1] Webster's Universal Dictionary & Thesaurus (Scotland, UK, Geddes & Grosset, 2005)

especially a response that has been subject to reinforcement or a conditioned response[2]

From these two definitions, we draw some lessons namely;

a. Habits are neither singular nor haphazard actions but regular and consistent manners of life. For instance, we all have the habit of waking up at a particular time in the morning. It is an accumulation of actions that occur over a period of time. The result is that one is an early-riser while the other is late.

b. Habits can become automatic responses (without thinking) to particular stimuli. For example, driving can become an automatic set of consistent actions that occur after one has learnt to drive. Initially, the learner used to be very conscious and even anxious about driving. However, through regular practice and acquisition of skills, driving becomes automatic (less conscious).

c. Habits are conditioned responses (fixed ways of responding to fixed stimuli) For example, when faced with danger, people respond according to the fixed way they are used to – flight or fight.

---

[2] Andrew M. Colman, *Oxford Dictionary of Psychology (Oxford University Press, New York:2006)*

d. Habits are peculiar to different people. People may face similar situations but will likely respond differently. For example, two persons may respond to a smiling face in divergent ways.

e. Habits are synonymous with attitudes or lifestyles. When actions congregate in a regular way, they are referred to as attitude or habit.

Stubborn Habits

Habits can be strong or weak, stubborn or amenable. When a habit is stubborn, it means that it is difficult to get rid of or deal with. For instance, I once had a roommate who could never empty his bowels in the morning until he had smoked. Try as he would to perform this natural and normal exercise, he couldn't until he had performed the ritual of smoking. For him, it is "no smoking, no bowel emptying." Consequently, smoking had become his own stubborn habit; just as the misuse of hard drugs was the stubborn habit of the former lecturer in an American University we mentioned earlier. As we can see, stubborn habits relate to negative and evil events of life. When habits are positive, we refer to them as being passionate.

Habits Or Attitudes

Like we said earlier, habits are synonymous with attitudes. They are peculiar and regular ways or mannerisms which vary from person to person. A few examples of the axioms of habits or attitudes include;

a. *I am convinced that life is ten percent what happens to me and ninety percent how I react to it.*[3]

b. *The greatest discovery of my generation is that people can change their lives by changing their attitude – William James.*[4]

c. *Attitude, more than aptitude, determines peoples altitude*[5]

When an action or behaviour gets to the level of habit or attitude, it becomes really serious. It is like arriving at the top of a huge mountain. Quality time and resources would have been expended.

The trajectory of habit formation begins with words. Words are the raw materials of every visible and invisible entity or phenomenon on earth and eternity. Consider this crucial structure of human destiny.

The structure of Destiny[6]

---

[3] Charles Swindoll in Zig Ziglar, *Over The Top* (Spiritual Life Outreach, Inc. Port Harcourt, Nigeria:2003)

[4] William James, Brainy Quote.com.xplore Inc. (https://www.brainquote.com Accessed January 18, 2017)

[5] Passy Amaraegbu, *The Eagle Generation* (Canniff Trust Ltd., Owerri, Nigeria: 1997)

Sow character and reap a Destiny.
Sow habit and reap character
Sow an action and reap a habit
Sow an emotion and reap an action
Sow a fact or truth and reap an emotion
Sow a thought and reap a fact or truth
Sow an idea and reap a thought
Sow a word and reap an idea

This structure of human destiny is a combined product of the famous American Psychologist, William James (1948) and Nigerian Psychologist Passy Amaraegbu (1995). The former's postulation involved the three topmost steps (from action to habit to character to destiny) while the latter's envolved the earlier five steps.

The Arithmetic Of Attitude

Someone used alphabets and made an interesting discovery about attitude. Assigning numbers to the alphabets, A to Z as 1 to 26, it was discovered that attitude sums up to 100. Let us apply the lesson to some terms or words.

a. Success (S=19, U=21, C=3, E=5) sums up to 94

---

[6]Passy Amaraegbu (2005) *Transforming Your Mind for Exploits Egbeda*, Lagos: Nigeria. Change Business Services Ltd.

b. Excellence = 88

c. Best = 46

d. Attitude = 100

There may not be too many words or terms that sum up to hundred. This is very intriguing. It strengthens the notion that our attitude is the complete and best signpost of our lives. We are our attitudes. Once we form them, they end up controlling us.

Consequently, we should be careful about the attitudes or habits we yield ourselves to. We must identify the attitudes or habits which drive our lives.

Habits as Signposts of lives

A signpost is a pole which gives direction or information about routes and distances. Habits are so significant in the lives of people that they stand as signposts which announce our personalities. Think of anybody you know, and you will recall two major traits about them, namely; their character (habits) and charisma (abilities, gifts).

An African proverb has it that, great accomplishment or achievement is the distinguishing nature of every famous personality. Literally, this means that, the degree of honour bestowed on people is directly proportional to the value they add to other people's lives. Consider these examples of people's signposts.

a. He is usually patient and understanding.

b. He is sold out to defend the weak and needy.

c. Her joyful lifestyle is infectious.

d. For more than a decade, I have known Anderline, she never comes late to meetings or appointments.

These examples, succinctly, highlight the fact that habits are signposts or roadmaps of our lives. We relate with others as well as others do to us based on our habits. Once they are formed, habits make or mar us. This is why we should be careful in choosing our habits or attitudes.

Summary

Light will always overpower darkness. This first chapter, focused on bringing clarity to the meaning of Stubborn Habit and its features. As a foundational chapter, understanding stubborn habits places a crucial role in dealing with the challenges and barriers such ignoble habits pose. Welcome to the worthy exercise of reading this book.

Personal Reflection

1. In your own words, how would you define stubborn habits?

_____

_____

_____

2. Is there any new knowledge you have gained from this introductory chapter and what is it?

_____

_____

_____

3. What is the relationship between personal habits and fulfillment of personal destiny?

_____

_____

_____

Chapter Two

CHARACTERISTICS OF STUBBORN HABITS

Like a nagging hag
As an untoward visitor
Stubborn habits hook us
Like deadly hookworms
They resist every attack
Rendering our armoury useless
Enslaving the brightest mind
Intoxicating the basest senses
Like caffeine they are addictive
As parasites they are poisonous
Competing against our progress
Compelling us to submission
Beaten and battered but not bowed
We cease the second chance to win.

It was a Sunday afternoon on the usual busy Lagos road. We were returning from a Service where I ministered, when suddenly I noticed a familiar face. After some hesitation, I summoned up courage to call his name. When he drew near, we stopped and chatted. I was correct that he was one of my High School classmates.

Twenty years after we left High School, he had neither advanced beyond that level of education nor acquired any useful skill. He was still feeding from hand to mouth. The story began far much earlier.

It began in our High School years in the seventies. A brilliant and articulate youth then, he was assailed by late-coming and absenteeism from school. Inspite of the harsh discipline meted on him due to these double degenerative habits, my former classmate refused to turn over a new leaf. He was incorrigible. He was stuck in the mud. He was hoodwinked. The long term consequence of these double shameful habits was a life of mediocrity and misery. The last time I saw him, he was also an addicted smoker. From this story of stubborn habits, we can draw some characteristics such as;

a. Deceptiveness
b. Debasing
c. Destruction.
d. Momentary Gratification
e. Peculiarity
f. Potency
g. Persistence
h. Pressurizing
i. Punitiveness
j. Problematic.

Let us consider these features briefly:

Deceptiveness

Like an enemy army, a stubborn habit begins with gaining a foothold through subtlety. Deception tells you that a little involvement in stubborn habit isn't harmful. It tells you that everybody is a victim of the evil habit. It will entice and seduce you to believe a lie. But remember that a little leaven, leavens the whole lump. The yeast that enlarges the bread is normally little compared to the size of the flour. Winning the war against stubborn habits begins with understanding this principle.

Debases

Imagine a healthy 21 year old young man regularly scaling a 14-feet fence into a Rehabilitation centre for the purpose of having sex with insane women.[7] According to him, he had been to this venue earlier on as a job applicant. An extreme case indeed but it is typical of stubborn habits. They are shameful and despicable. They are bestial and debasing.

Destruction

If not arrested, stubborn habits will end up destroying the victim. The destruction affects every aspect of life. Consider the pitiable stories of many celebrities who die bankrupt; some musicians who die as drug addicts; many great men and women who end up poorly and sadly. The root cause of most of these terrible endings is stubborn habits. People pay dearly for allowing negative habits to dominate their lives.

---

[7] Guardian Newspaper Limited, (Lagos; Nigeria: 5, August 2013:13)

Momentary Gratification

All forms of evil are rich in euphoria. Evil seduces. The search for gratification is the backbone of evil. Consider the brief tickling and teasing of fleshly pleasures, the momentary elation of self glorification, the tintinabulation of lecherous expression.

Stubborn habits offer stupendous opportunities of momentary gratification. But like smoke, they will always vanish.

Peculiarity

No two individuals manifest the same depth and degree of stubborn habits. The nomenclature and normative may be similar but vary in degree or magnitude. Alcoholism, pilfering, lying, or any other bad habit exist in diverse degrees in different people. Furthermore, different people are victims of different forms of stubborn habits. Some may be more disposed to telling lies in some aspects of their lives than the others. This may be in business, marriage, academics, institution, etcetera.

Some families; societies and institutions permit some evil habits. For example, what stubborn habits are some African governments known for? Inability to raise effective successors. What of American government? The role of a domineering world police. Can you identify your own peculiar stubborn habit?

Potency

Why would someone become a victim to an evil lifestyle or a captive to an evil habit? Why would one hate, cry against and regret engaging in a habit but engage in it again? Why would a dog return to its vomit?

> *Now if I do what I will not to do, it is not longer I who do it, but sin that dwells in me. I find then a law, that evil is present with me, the one who wills to do good.*[8]

Stubborn habits have controlling power. They tend to take over the victim's will and mind and dictate what behavioural pattern to follow or refrain from. There are doctors who are treating HIV patients who still engage in sexual promiscuity or those treating alcoholic cirrhosis who are still drunkards. There are lawyers helping criminals who are habitual law-breakers. Stubborn habits are indeed potent.

Persistence

If it isn't persistent, then it isn't a habit. Like sick people, victims of stubborn habits must regularly engage in the evil habit. The body and mind have become accustomed to and enslaved by that habit. In fact, they are expectant and desirous of receiving the stimulus. The body and mind have reached the

---

[8] Romans 7:20,21

level whereby they are craving for stimulation. Stubborn habits are persistent.

Pressurizing
Stubborn habits put a lot of pressure on the individual. The pressure can be physical, psychological and spiritual. Drug addiction is a typical case of a stubborn habit which can exert unusual and extreme pressure on the victim. The psychological pressures of drug addiction persist after the physical has subsided. This is why the right treatment should be multi-dimensional; such as; – medical, psychological and spiritual. One drug addict, after wasting all his financial resources on hard drugs, equally stole the money his wife gave him to feed their baby and used it to satisfy the craving for drugs

Punitiveness
Stubborn habits are punitive. They unleash punishments on their victims. Consider the case of unbridled spousal violence. In the process of assaulting a spouse, the assailant can become an accident victim. For instance, he can fall down or suffer a humiliating revenge from the victim.

Furthermore, stubborn habits demand a higher investment of psychological energy as well as other resources.

Problematic

Stubborn habits create enormous problems for the victims and their significant others. Those who engage in Internet pornography, for instance, open the door of their lives to other sexual dysfunctional problems such as unbridled control of their libido, inability to engage in normal and healthy sexual relationship, poor productive living, excetera.

Summary

Engaging in stubborn habits is consequential. It may offer some benefits but the consequences surpass the benefits. A proper assessment of these consequences can enable one to rise up and wage war against stubborn habits.

Personal Reflection

1. Based on the information obtained from this chapter, differentiate between weak and stubborn habits.

   _____

   _____

2. Which characteristics of stubborn habits is most significant to you and why?

   _____

   _____

3. What other characteristics of these stubborn habits have manifested in your life which were not mentioned/listed here?

_____

_____

Chapter Three

PORTRAITS OF STUBBORN HABITS

Sometime in 2011, I was one of the international students of Bakke Graduate University who attended a two-week intensive academic and practical doctoral programme in Ghana. Participants were drawn from Africa, Europe, Asia and America. The picture of the Professor of Records we saw on the Internet was that of a youngman. However, when I got to Accra, Ghana and moved to the hotel which served both as residence for some students and lecturers as well as venue of the programme, I was amazed by the contact I had with Dr. Randy White, the Professor of Records. First, was his exemplary character which was manifested in humility, kindness and sacrificial love for others. Here was a man who travelled hundreds of kilometers and flew for several hours coming all the way from USA who should be tired and relaxing, meeting the students at the hotel lobby and helping us to settle down. Infact, I struggled to prevent him from helping me with my luggage but he prevailed. Again, he looked older than his picture I saw on the Internet. So, I learnt that pictures or portraits might not be entirely accurate all the time. At other times, they are the true image of the person.

So we ask, what are the true portraits of stubborn habits? What is our perception of stubborn habits? Do our perceptions correlate negatively or positively with stubborn habits? Are there some commonalities with stubborn habits? Yes, there are. These commonalities can be seen in the following portraits.

a. Parasitic Relationship
b. Poison in the system
c. Untoward visitor
d. Inflammation/Infection
e. Weed in the farm
f. Malignant wound

Let us consider these in some detail:

Parasitic Relationship

Stubborn habits, like parasites, inhabit and feed on the host (victim of the habit). Outside the host, their survival is almost impossible.

Consequently, stubborn habits are harmful to their hosts. They weaken and weary, deplete and endanger the energy of the host as well as deny the host essential benefits. They compete against the well being and welfare of the host. They encumber the host as well as endanger his/her health. The depth of parasitic indwelling can be so profound that when the untoward visitor is eliminated, the host experiences temporary comatose. This is comparable to the case of serious drug addiction whereby effort to wean the victim from the stubborn habit is frustrated by contrary and habitual physiological, chemical as well as psycho-spiritual forces.

Poison in the System

All that is needed to poison any meal is to add a little quantity of the death-solvent or solution. With regard to food poisoning, the axiom which espouses that a little leaven leavens the lump is apt. Consequently, a stubborn habit is like poison which destroys the system that accommodates it. Think of the immeasurable harm a habit like worry or anxiety does to the lives of people. High blood pressure and other diseases of the nervous system are some of the products of being worrisome and anxious.

Furthermore, consider the damaging impact of another stubborn habit like nagging. Under the influence of a nagging spouse, a man or woman may fall victim to various accidents, become a victim of another stubborn habit like drunkenness, philandering or spousal violence.

Untoward Visitor

We are familiar with the invasion of an unwanted visitor. Take for instance, when one is due for an appointment and suddenly such a visitor invades one's private world. It causes unnecessary disruption of plans, psychological disequilibrium, as well as wastage of resources and time. Stubborn habits are detestable invaders of our organized world. They aim at assailing and attacking our productive schedules. They are selfish and harmful.

Thief in the Night

A thief is different from a robber. While the former is subtle and secretive, the latter is bold and boisterous. A stubborn habit is like a thief, who strikes at an unsuspecting season or moment. He is an opportunist who desires to operate in secrecy or under cover. Consider the fact that victims of various stubborn habits are evasive and self-protective. They always seek to rationalize their error and end up covering what should be exposed and expunged. This is a proof that they are under the influence of a thief. It takes some sober reflection and search through one's house (life) to discover the damage done by a thief. Initially one may assume that all is well until further analysis is carried out. A stubborn habit is like a thief in the night.

An Inflammation

One effect of infection is inflammation. The cell, organ or system is under attack. Harmful micro-organisms like bacteria, fungi or virus invade the body and cause significant damage. Consider cases like filariasis or elephantiasis. Both are inflammatory diseases caused by the introduction of germs called filariae.

In the same manner, the appendix in the human body under infection becomes inflamed and must be cut off, otherwise, it spells doom for the victim. A stubborn habit is like an inflamed appendix. The longer it stays, the more dangerous it becomes. It takes courage to cut it off. Stop it before it stops you.

Weed in the Farm

Weeds can easily be mistaken for plants or crops because they sometimes resemble the latter. Yet, they are dangerous competitors and actual enemies of the crop. They compete for air, water, space and nutrient. They are so vicious and dangerous that they may end up usurping all the necessary resources for the growth and development of the crop.

Stubborn habits are exactly like weeds in the farmland. They compete against the crops for every resource. For instance, consider the strain and stress of a stubborn habit like adult enuresis (bedwetting).

The prevalence of enuresis decreases with age. As many as 10 percent of children who are 5 years suffer from this disorder, compared to 3 to 5 percent of 10years olds and 1 percent of 15year olds.[9]

This singular habit can drain all the energy and attention of a victim. It can assume the identity of the individual and cause stigmatization. It can rob

---

[9] America Psychiatric Association, 2000, *America Psychiatric Association,* 2000, DSM-IV text Revision, Washington, D.C.)

one of every zeal and zest, confining the victim to a wretched lifestyle.

A malignant wound

A stubborn habit is like a malignant wound which produces a terrible odour. Like a putrefying sore, a stubborn habit is the source of excruciating pain as well as tormenting emotions. It limits one's mobility, frustrates efforts towards progress and endangers one's health.

Take a case of habitual shoplifting for an example. The day the thief is caught becomes his/her waterloo. Even if the habit goes on unnoticed and unannounced, it neither diminishes the degree of personal embarrassment nor the consequences of personal ineptitude.

Summary

In any way or manner one views a stubborn habit, the conclusion is that it is an evil wind which bestows neither benefit nor blessing. It is an unnecessary burden to bear, a wasteful lifestyle to maintain and an unprofitable business to engage in.

Personal Reflection

1. Write down the portraits of Stubborn Habits you identify with and why?

_____

_____

_____

2. Does the knowledge of the nefarious nature of stubborn habits motivate you to resolve to win the battle over them? If yes, to what extent. If no, why not?

_____

_____

_____

Chapter Four

DEVELOPMENTAL STAGES OF STUBBORN HABITS

One of the characteristics of organisms (living things) is that they grow. They make progress and don't remain stagnant. Habits possess life and therefore grow from one stage to the other. We shall use two illustrations to convey this lesson. These are the development of strongholds and the life of a plant.

First Approach: Development of Strongholds.

Stronghold is a military term which depicts a fortress, a centre of strength or support. Normally when two warring groups or nations enter the battle field, they designate a clear-cut boundary. Each occupies a specific territory with clearly marked boundaries. As the battle progresses, one of the nations or groups will end up giving or yielding up a part of her territory. Usually, this starts in small measures. Consider these diagrammes.

Diagrammes of Foot and Strongholds.

Figure I

A	C	B

Note:- A and B show two nations at war
C represents Territorial boundary

Figure II

A	C	B

Note:- A and B show two nations at war
C represents new territorial boundary with the Foothold of nation B on A.

And do not give the devil a foothold[10]

Foothold is the small but significant territorial gain of an enemy over the opponent. As small as it is, a foothold is remarkably consequential. In statistical terminology, a foothold is significant.

It is important because it represents:

---

[10] Eph.4:27 (NIV)

- The first evidence of the superiority of one group or nation over the other.
- A little leaven (yeast) that leavens the whole lump.
- It is a symbol of victory.
- Foothold offers the enemy a great opportunity to launch attack from within and no longer from outside.
- It strengthens the enemy to launch more dangerous attacks while weakening the opponent.

Now how does this relate to stubborn habits? Stubborn habits begin like footholds-small, sure-footed and within the territory of the opponent. Consider any stubborn habit you know. The beginning is normally small but if allowed, it will grow bigger and stronger. Spousal violence, bitterness, drug addiction, kleptomania, paedophilia, anorexia nervosa, vaginismus, et cetera.

However, with persistence pressure and time, the little horn develops into a huge one; the foothold develops into a stronghold. It is a major fortress or warehouse of military armour belonging to an assailant or enemy within one's territorial boundary. It signifies:

- Progressive Victory
- Enemy Mastery
- Internal invasion

- Consolidated and successful territorial expansion
- Consequently, the existence of an enemy's stronghold spells more doom for any group or nation. It is easier to deal with a foot than a stronghold.

In the same manner, it is easier to deal with a stubborn habit at the early stage than at the latter stage. One of the characteristics of stubborn habits is that they are degenerative. As time goes on, the condition goes from bad to worse and to worst. The habit becomes addictive. In the case of drug addiction, smaller quantities that used to produce the euphoric effects may no longer suffice. The result is that the victim will be forced to ingest more quantity (or dosage) of the drug in order to obtain the usual euphoric experience.

A second way to consider the development of stubborn habits is from the viewpoint of a farmer who is seriously engaged in the business of sowing and reaping. He begins with obtaining the precious seed.

Second Approach: Crop Production
Someone rightly noted that inside a viable seed, is the life of a forest. Every farmer appreciates the value of a viable seed. He knows that without the seed, there will be no crop and therefore, no harvest. In relation to stubborn habit, the seed is the first or initial content of the habit (initial

stimulus). For instance, the seed of promiscuity was sown in a teenage boy through sexual childhood abuse by the housemaid; or the stealing seed sown in a secondary school boy whom robbery was the source of his father's wealth.

The life of a crop can be divided into five phase viz: *planting, seedling, maturity, fruiting and declining.* The planting stage of stubborn habit is the beginning period when the individual is exposed to the stimulus which provokes the habit. Let us use addiction to Internet pornography as an example. What provokes this stubborn habit? The relevant provocative stimuli may include, association with an addict, loneliness, laziness or joblessness.

The next stage should be the seedling period when the seed begins to germinate and grow. In relationship to stubborn habit, the seed of pornography begins to exert pressure and influence on the victim. In this stage, the event is still in the short-term memory. Early and repetitive reinforcement of the stimulus strengthens the conditioning of the stubborn behaviour. Contrariwise, delayed action and irregularity of the stimulus, weakens as well as hinders the repetition of the behaviour. This is a conducive stage to break the stubborn habit. Imagine the stretching of the taproot and other roots of the seedling into the soil in order to achieve balance, obtain nutrient and water for growth and health. In like manner, at this second stage, the new habit will begin to make impact in the memory, thought pattern and emotion of the victim. It will begin to create its own memory record and pathway by stirring up both biochemical and psycho-spiritual reactions. If not arrested, this stubborn habit will grow and develop to the maturity stage.

The maturity stage is marked by certain characteristics like consolidation, stability, potency, viability, viciousness, contagiousness and productivity or multiplicity. At this stage, the habit has been ingrained in the three levels of memory-short, mid and long term. Now, it rightly assumes the status of a stubborn habit. It becomes the name tag, nickname or nomenclature of the individual. At this stage, the habit has attained notoriety.

Fruiting or crop production is the next stage. Like the term suggests, this stage is marked by the production of fruits or its kind. As usual, maturity precedes the fruit-bearing stage. In relation to stubborn habit, this is the period during which the habit becomes complex and manifests in other diverse ways producing its own kind. Using the example of indulgence in pornography we mentioned earlier, the offsprings would include; secrecy, wastage of time, lustful thinking, lying, or hypocrisy. Biochemical and psycho-spiritual activities and reactions reach their zenith at this stage of the development of the stubborn habit. Equally, the habit becomes a case of public concern. In the real sense of the word, both the victim and people around him will begin to habour doubts on the ability of the victim to conquer the habit. Also, it is such a dangerous period in the life of the victim that if nothing is done to assist him deal with the situation, he will pay dearly for it in terms of poisoning personal relationships, crippling career and business opportunities, and endangering success in life. Of course, all these are rooted in spiritual decline. The victim may end up in self-destructive actions. At other times, the habit, like an old tree which has survived many seasons as well as exhausted its fruiting capacity, begins to experience a natural death. Most often, the terrible consequences of the habit is the precursor of this decline in potency. The stubborn habit would have created so much trouble for the victim that he would be desirous to detach from it. Normally, at sober moments, the victim, through reflection and meditation desires to quit the stubborn habit; but like a faulty old gramophone, may return and repeat the former sound. Unable to help oneself or obtain help from others, the victim may end up in personal or public imprisonment. The talkativeness may lead to violence which may lead to physical damage or incarceration or death.

Here, are the five stages of the development of stubborn habits and their features.

The life Span of Stubborn Habits

S/N	STAGE	FEATURES
1.	Sowing	a. Onset of Stubborn Habit b. Level of conditioning depends on the potency of content. c. Short memory
2.	Seedling	a. Fast growth or death of habit. b. Strong battle for existence. c. Exertion of pressure to survive.
3.	Maturity	a. Consolidation b. Establishment of pattern. c. Access to three levels of memory. (Short, mid and long term) d. Beginning of stigmatization
4.	Fruiting	a. Massive productive activities. b. Multiplication of similar habits. c. Complexity in nature. d. Establishment of stigmatization. e. Domination of all levels of memory.
5.	Decline	a. Weakness of the habit b. Development of guilt c. Inner cry for help d. Consequences reach Zenith degree.

NB: Victory over stubborn habit can occur at any of these stages. However, the earlier, the better and easier.

Summary

46

This chapter is instructive. Using the two approaches of the development of stubborn habits, each of us has to examine ourselves to determine our involvement with stubborn habits. Are we victims? Are we at the foot or stronghold stage? Or at the different five levels of the life of a plant?

This assessment will facilitate our seeking and obtaining help to overcome stubborn habits.

Personal Reflection

1. Clearly identify the new pieces of information you have gained from this chapter.

   _____

   _____

   _____

2. Which of the two approaches that show the developmental stages of stubborn habits resonates with you and why?

   _____

   _____

   _____

Chapter Five

FOUNDATIONS OF STUBBORN HABITS

It was 1977. We were young teenage pioneers in a Boys Secondary School in Eziachi, Orlu, Imo State, Nigeria. We had just returned from the long vocation and were preparing to begin our second year academic work in earnest. Coming from the village and with less exposure to industrial development, I listened with rapt attention as my more privileged classmates narrated stories of city life and enjoyment. In the midst of this reverie, my eyes caught attention of the book one of them was holding. Out of curiosity I requested to see the book. He obliged and in a few minutes, I was lost as I began with the blurb and not long after, I was devouring the book. This was the first James Hardley Chase novel I read. From that time, I got hooked to the series. The Hardley Chase series celebrated crime and immorality. Consequently, I read all the titles I came across. Equally, I went in search of others; and though this habit never endangered my academic pursuit, it became my major preoccupation during the holiday. Years after, this habit tested and tried my resolve to break it.

This example highlights one of the avenues through which stubborn habits gain access to people's lives-curiosity. It is the act of desiring and daring to know. Curiosity can lead one to positive or negative actions. While curiosity is common among youths, it isn't limited to them. Other door-ways to stubborn habits include;

a. Inheritance
b. Peer Group pressure
c. Hard drugs
d. Indiscipline
e. Evil communication
f. Faulty Parenting
g. Carnal Nature
h. Demonic influence

Inheritance

There are two views on this matter. First is the idea that, just as we inherit our genetic components, we also inherit character traits.

The second one is that habits are learned behaviours and cannot be inherited. Each of us determines what to learn or choose to acquire.

These two views represent the traditional nature-versus-nurture opposing stand. The solution is a midway approach whereby nature provides the tendency and nurture determines the degree of manifestation of the habit. Let us take an example using the smoking habit. Though there is no genetic trait responsible for smoking, a smoker-mother naturally empowers her foetus to crave for smoking than a non-smoker mother. The food nutrients which pass through the placenta to the foetus have significant evidence of nicotine in them, which can make the child more vulnerable to smoking habit than the child of a non-smoking mother. Also, a smoking mother provides a conducive environment (nurture) for the development of this habit among the members of her home. This is through vicarious learning and socialization. Therefore, we conclude that stubborn habits can be the product of the interplay of nature and nurture.

Peer group pressure
None of us lives for ourselves. We are all the products of diverse influences. Particularly during the adolescent period, the human person is susceptible to pressures from colleagues, and classmates, friends and foes as well. Many young people end up becoming victims of negative peer pressure. The reasons for this include, inadequate or poor parenting, the youths' desire to please others, uncertainty about or ignorance of the truth, the desire to belong or be accepted in the group.

Peer group pressure goes beyond the adolescent period and is a significant doorway through which many people are enslaved to stubborn habits. People have joined occultic groups, broken marital vows, reneged on their sacred commitments or engaged in some other shameful behaviours because of peer group pressure. Each of us must discover what is right and determine to stand by it inspite of peer group pressure.

Hard drugs

Involvement in hard drugs is problematic. Such an involvement can predispose the victim to break laws or begin the journey on the road to stubborn habit. For instance, alcoholism, an example of stubborn habit can predispose the victim to marital violence. It becomes the situation that anytime the man gets drunk, he exhibits intimate partner violence (IPV).

One of the characteristics of hard drugs is the distortion of reality which comes through altering the state of one's consciousness. The result is underrating or exaggerating events, people, circumstances and situations. Therefore, involvement in hard drugs can predispose someone to becoming a victim of stubborn habits.

Indiscipline

By nature, mankind tends to gravitate towards indiscipline. This is why we say that to err is human, to forgive is divine. We crave for pleasure and self-gratification rather than yield to self-control and self-denial. Hedonism, gluttony, alcoholism, and every other stubborn habit are the products of an indisciplined lifestyle.

Evil communication

Besides the issue of peer pressure, several people become victims of stubborn habits through the activities of friends. Evil communication truly corrupts good manners.[11]

Faulty parenting

Parenting is a serious business. Only few couples prepare for it before the arrival of their children. Most stubborn habits have both their foundation and their building blocks laid at home. Faulty parenting methods like polygamy, singular parenting, absentee parenting, dysfunctional and laissez faire parenting; all fester the evolution of stubborn habits. Several occasions abound where the parents or either of them is a victim of stubborn habits. How can such parents help a child who has a similar challenge?

Carnal Nature

As fishes survive and thrive in the water so do stubborn habits in an atmosphere of carnality or worldliness. The tendencies of the uncontrolled human nature are: immorality, filthiness, indecent actions, idol worship, witchcraft practices, envy, jealousy, anger, divisiveness, and their likes. Carnality or the lifestyle of the old nature is a major reason why many believers fall victim to stubborn habits. The decision to live in the spirit will release one from the captivating influence of stubborn habits.

---

[11] *1Cor. 15:33*

Demonic Influence
The powers of darkness can provoke and sustain stubborn habits. The master trickster and deceiver the devil, and his demons can lure people to engage in horrible habits. Consider a case of kleptomania. This is an impulsive stubborn habit which results in repeated stealing of objects which aren't needful to the individual. Why would one keep stealing things he or she doesn't need? Why expose oneself to unnecessary shame and reproach? Why should somebody endanger oneself by engaging in pilfering? It is either a sign of insanity or demonic control.

Summary
Foundations are very important in life. They determine the capacity and strength of physical structures as well as organisms. Understanding the foundation of stubborn habits will enhance every effort to handle them.

Personal Reflection

1. Based on the knowledge you have gained from this chapter, what is (are) likely the taproot(s) of stubborn habits in your life?

_____

_____

_____

2. Which foundational root stands out most significantly to you and why?

_____

_____

_____

Chapter Six

PROMOTERS OF STUBBORN HABITS

It is a common event to see a conflagration lose its fervency. Either of these things will happen; the fire will die down or it will be fanned into flame again. Habits are like that. No matter how stubborn or gratifying they are, a victim at one point or the other will grow weary of the habit. On the other hand, the stubborn habit can wear the victim out.

Promoters of stubborn habits are circumstances and situations which fan the embers of habits to flame. They feed the habits. They are the building blocks of stubborn habits. The avenues are primary or foundation stones while the promoters are the secondary or building blocks. These promoters include;

a. A pervading corrupt culture
b. A compromised Media
c. An evolving Apathetic Neighbourhood.
d. The lure of Technological opportunities
e. The reign of humanism
f. Bad Role Models.
g. Systemic Evil.

Pervading Corrupt Culture

Culture simply means the way of life of a people. It includes their values, language, dressing, diet and worldview. In our contemporary world, in spite of the diversity of our tribes and races; there exist some common values or worldviews which cut across board. One of such common features of our modern day culture which promotes the development of stubborn habits is inconsistency of standard of living among custodians of our culture. Inconsistency of lifestyle and language, ineptitude and indiscipline which flow from the head deals a devastating blow on the system. The result is corruption and weakening of the system. For instance, most cultures pretend to uphold fidelity in marriage but indirectly cherish and sponsor diverse programmes which frustrate marital chastity such as fertility festivals, immoral carnival and their bikes. Most cultures desire to eat their cakes and still have them. This hypocritical lifestyle promotes the evolution and sustenance of stubborn habits.

A Compromised Media
Driven by the Machiavellian philosophy of the end justifying the means, most businesses in our contemporary world particularly those using various media apparatus, have succumbed to compromised standards. A few examples may suffice. Why engage in lavish cigarette advertisement without providing adequate warning for the audience of the imminent health hazards inherent in the habit? Why promote pornography on television and turn around to demand chastity from people? Why invest millions of dollars into immoral projects but refuse to invest into projects that will benefit the populace such as

education, economic empowerment and eradication of diseases? The obvious answer is that corrupt and evil businesses appear more profitable than the ones that promote human nobility and virtue. This is so because these vices appeal to the carnal nature of man.

An Apathetic Neighbourhood

Apathy is one of the consequences of technological advancement. Today, most of us care more for the safety of our machines than we do for fellow humans. These modern toys have become the measuring rods of our lives. For instance, someone rightly noted that most men spend more time and money on their cars than they do on their wives.

Other examples of wickedness in human relationship abound. Accident victims on our roads are abandoned to fate. Robbery and rape, occultic and gang invasions go on uninterrupted in our neighbourhoods because neighbours neither care nor are touched by the afflictions of others. Children and wards wallow in misdemeanour and misconducts in the full glare of elders, friends and neighbours and they are neither reported to their parents nor disciplined by the witnesses. Indeed, any human left alone to do what pleases him or her will likely end up in the pigestry.

In the past, African culture forbade any form of open misdemeanour or evil. Africans lived a community-sensitive life. An African proverb has it that a child is fostered by a cluster or team of elders. The increase in the divorce rate in our society today is an eloquent evidence of the breakdown of community life.

Lure of Technological Gadgets.

Technology came with immense benefits and blessings. Yet, it is laden with curses and callousness. Consider these ugly examples of the misuse of technology;

a. A marriage engagement ended because the few occasions a man visited the future wife, he was glued to his laptop and had little or no time for discussion or interaction.
b. A ten-year old marriage is in crisis because the husband is enslaved to Internet pornography.
c. An intelligent law undergraduate is about to be sent out of the university because his interest in computer games is destroying his academic opportunities.
d. A celebrated international athlete has gone bankrupt because of his unbridled love for new cars (auto mania)

Reign of Humanism

Psychology is not just a significant aspect of human life in our globe; it is the centre point of modern life. In our contemporary world, humanistic psychology is the reigning school of thought. It postulates and propounds that individual free-will and self actualization are the sacred tenets of human development and harmony.

One of the consequences of this school of thought is that every dysfunctional behaviour is viewed within the prism of personal development. In other words, neither individuals nor institutions have the authority to intervene in anybody's lifestyle. Everybody should be allowed to develop into their unique personality. Conformity to norms, allegiance to corporate responsibility are all sacrificed at the altar of selfish pursuits. When the rule is neither intervene nor interfere with another person's life, the product will be a massive evolution of dysfunctional lifestyles. Of course, stubborn habits like a river with several tributaries will flood the land.

Evil Role Models

A society that promotes evil, honours men and women with inept character, celebrates those who thrive on vices; but despises those with noble character is bound for destruction. Most people easily learn from our manners than from our messages. Undergraduates on campus may criticize inept politicians, but given opportunity to govern they end up worse. Apprentices may detest the corrupt lifestyles of their principals but may never offer better services. The reason is that bad example lingers more than the good. Weak human nature craves and easily finds partnership with bad example than the good. We all remember evil events and occurrences but tend to forget the good quickly. Evil role models fan the flame of stubborn habits to the hilt.

Systemic Evil
When evil becomes entrenched in a society or system, it is referred to as systemic. For instance, in governance, the executive may conspire with the legislature and the judiciary to perpetuate injustice, tribalism or other forms of ineptitude. In the business world, manufacturers or producers conspire with the wholesale marketers and the retailers to trade on expired, low quality or fake products. Systemic evil promotes stubborn habits to a large degree.

Summary
In examining the issues which promote stubborn habits in the lives of people, we noted that they are diverse and pervasive in our contemporary society. We need to dispassionately consider the impact of each of them in our lives so that we can seek for help.

Personal Reflection

1. What factors exercabate the influence of stubborn habits in your life?

   _____

   _____

2. In practical ways, what can you do to remove such negative influences in your life?

_____

_____

Chapter Seven

THE CHALLENGE OF RECIDIVISM

On February 6, 1983 while attending a Charismatic Students Fellowship at Saint Peter's Catholic Chapel of the University of Nigeria, Nsukka, I received the New Life in Christ Jesus. One major sinful habit that assailed me was sexual lust. At almost 19years, I was a virgin but lustful thoughts did terrible damage to my soul. Obtaining the new life in Christ was really wonderful and transforming. My soul was filled with joy as I gained total forgiveness and liberty from the power of lust of the eyes and flesh.

However, one year after, I lost this joy of the new life as I began to backslide into the old sinful habit of entertaining lustful thoughts. A major reason why I experienced backsliding was distraction from spiritual matters. I got involved in Students Union politics which made extra demand on my time. Consequently, I had little or no time for personal devotion.

Honestly, I have experienced other forms of backsliding since 1984 but grace has always enabled me to return to my first love for God.

This story connects with the theme of this chapter. Recidivism refers to the tendency of a law-breaker to commit the offence again.[12] It is a relapse tendency into criminal activities.[13]

Perhaps no victim of stubborn habits is totally free from recidivism. It is a huge challenge to everybody who has been involved in stubborn habits. Smokers and smugglers, robbers and ruffians, fornicators and fortune-tellers, liars and laggards, mercenaries and misers, assasins and arsonists, all fall prey to recidivism.

The proverbial wrong attitude to new year resolution is a metaphor of human recidivism. In less than a fortnight, many who engaged themselves in the practice of new year resolution end up as victims of what they renounced and rejected. The question is, why? Why is recidivism common among victims of stubborn habits? The reasons are diverse and may include the following:

a. Stubborn habits are pleasurable.
b. Stubborn habits form a chain reaction
c. Breaking stubborn habits are consequential
d. Stubborn habits thrive on corrupt association.
e. Stubborn habits have pscho-somatic connection.

The Lure of Pleasure
Engaging in stubborn habits provides the dividend of pleasure to the body, mind as well as emotion.

---

[12] https://www.google.com (Accessed 24/1/17)
[13] https://www.merriam-webeter.com/dictionary/recidivism (Accessed 24/1/17)

Hedonism is truly a strong driving force in life. Mortals naturally incline to what is pleasurable and profitable.

Therefore, victims of stubborn habits may succumb to the habit when they consider the pleasure they derive from engaging in it. Lot's wife might have been preoccupied with this hedonistic mindset when she stubbornly turned back to look at Sodom. The result was that she became a bag of salt[14]. She was unlike Moses whom it was said that,

> By faith Moses, when he became of age, refused to be called the son of Pharaoh's daughter choosing rather to suffer affliction with the people of God than to enjoy the pleasures of sin.[15]

No doubting the fact that stubborn habits attract the dividend of pleasure, yet this feeling is euphoric and actually consequential. Every victim of stubborn habit should follow Moses' example and starve it to death. Starving the habit involves making a resolute decision to deny oneself all the opportunities to engage or indulge in it. It is the process of self-denial as well as detachment from everything that connects one to the habit.

---

[14] Gen. 19:26
[15] Heb. 11:24,25

Stubborn Habits Exist in a Chain Reaction

Normally, what began as a simple action may develop into a complex web or repetitive activities. One authority states that it takes about twenty-one repetitive actions to form a habit.[16] Maxwell Maltz, a plastic surgeon is the proponent of this popular view which contemporarily in behavioural sciences is considered to be outdated.[17] Current researches show that it takes more than two months before a new behaviour becomes a habit (automatic). In fact, it takes exactly about 66days to form a new habit.[18]

Repeating the action causes some chain reactions. Some are psycho-spiritual while others are bio-chemical and psychosomatic. Those chain reactions reinforce recidivism. Like a drowning man, a stubborn habit that is undergoing pressures engages in a terrible battle of survival and may end up disrupting a lot of other life endeavours.

Stubborn habits are complex and complicated. This is part of the reason why they may reappear.

The Fear of Consequences

Breaking a stubborn habit can be consequential. Not many victims are prepared to pay the price of self-denial and crucifixion. For instance, a drug addict

---

[16] Jamesclear.com, *Behavioural Psychology*. "How long Does it Actually Take to Form a New Habit?" (Accessed February, 16,2017)
[17] Ibid Jamesclear.com
[18] Ibid Jamesclear.com

who is entirely cut off from his usual supply *(cold turkey treatment)* may become restless and violent until his demand for the supply of the drug is *met.*

Stubborn Habits Thrive on Corrupt Association

One of the strongest arguments about the prison system of every nation is that, is it a reformatory or conducive environment for recidivism? The reason being that many simple criminals return from the prison as hardened criminals.[19] One authority stated that 50-55% of state prisoners returned to prison within three to five years of their release.[20] Why?

Erroneously, many first time offenders are lodged together with hardened and worst offenders. At other times, those who are awaiting trial (AWT) are lodged with these capital offenders and the result is the corruption of the first offenders and civil crime breakers. The corrupt company ends up destroying the destiny of many. These simple or first time offenders when they are released from the prison now engage in worse and bigger crimes. And if nothing significantly different is done to interfere with the

---

[19] Passy Amaraegbu, The Nigerian Prison Sector Reform Conference "Behaviour Modification As a Significant Remedy for Recidivism Among Nigerian Prisoners" (Abuja: June 2015).
[20] Leon Neyfakh Why Do So Many Ex-Cons End Up Back to Prison? www.slate.com/articles/news_and_politics/crime/2015/10 (Accessed 25 January 2017).

cycle of criminal activities, the victims may die as criminals.

Psycho-Somatic Connection

The term psycho-somatic means, mind (psche) and body (soma). It deals with issues which concern both the mind and body. For instance, some sicknesses or diseases are referred to as psycho-somatic. These include, duedonal ulcer, depression, high blood pressure, and different heart and nervous diseases.

In the same manner, recidivism has a significant relationship with psycho-somatism. Normally, the mind determines the condition of the body. Our predominant thoughts and emotions are expressed through our bodies. The body is the servant of the mind.

Consequently, a mind that is set or determined to do good will be expressed through the body. The converse is also true.

Besides the spiritual dimension of human behaviour, the psychological aspect is very strong and significant. The human brain is comparable to the computer whose function can be summarised into three basic aspects of *encoding, storage* and *decoding.* It is a systematic device which operates as an input and output mechanism. Both the brain and computer need to be fed so that they can also release their products.

Consequently, if we feed our brain (the physical expression of the mind) with negative activities, the result will be that we will release negative products. If the brain gets used to responding to negative stimuli, it will become conditioned to such negative influences. This is referred to as conditioning or habituation and may lead to fixation. This phenomenon can be likened to muscle development. The human brain possesses a huge elastic capacity for development. Consequently, when the brain has developed the capacity to respond to a particular stimulus in a peculiar manner, it will maintain this trend or pattern until a stronger force compels it to act otherwise.

For the fact that the mind (brain) controls the body, the latter will respond to stimuli in the environment in accordance to the conditioned pattern and instruction it receives from the former. Hence, somebody who is used to (conditioned) responding to taking people's jewelry when left alone, will likely repeat the action on several occasions. Someone who is conditioned to violent actions will likely respond violently when he is provoked. This fixated behaviour is referred to as conditioned response. It actually explains why recidivism is common place.

However, human behaviour surpasses the realm of mind and body. We are endowed with greater capacities to break limitations. We can choose to react or respond. We have the power of choice. We shall consider this later in the book.

Summary

Understanding the thesis of this chapter will help one to be prepared to seek freedom. Each of us should desire and dare to break the chains of recidivism. We all can begin a revolution of regaining personal freedom.

Personal Reflection

1. From a personal perspective, do you think that it is possible to overcome the force of recidivism?

   _____

   _____

   _____

2. What can predispose you to recidivism and why?

   _____

   _____

   _____

3. What can you do to minimize or eradicate the effect of recidivism?

   _____

   _____

Chapter Eight

CONSEQUENCES OF STUBBORN HABITS

Besides being a prosperous businessman, Dan is also brilliant. However, he ended his education at the Secondary School level before going full swing into business. He was an apprentice for five years and within the next five years when he began his own motor spare parts business, it prospered greatly. Dan married Njideka, a Mass Communication graduate who initially worked in a private Television station but when the children began to arrive, accepted the husband's advice to resign and give full attention to parenting.

After two years of this arrangement, Dan began to complain that the cost of running the home was exorbitant and that Njideka was too sophisticated and greedy. When she requested to resume work, he refused and retorted that she should cut her coat according to her material. Njideka would laugh at such pieces of advice from her husband because she knew that both her demands and the cost of running the home were modest. She was sure that Dan was under some negative influences. She was aware of the various evil forces in the market-place such as occultic initiation, men's philandering attitude and various profiteering opportunities. She had tried a few times to discuss the matter with Dan but he wouldn't create time for the discussion.

It was a fateful Friday night in November and by 12.00pm Dan hadn't returned home. He normally returned home around 9.00pm and might be an half hour late if there was heavy traffic on the road or emergencies in the office. Njideka began to call Dan around 9.30pm but his two mobile phones were inaccessible. The two apprentices who worked for and lived with him returned to the house around 10.00pm and told their Madam that their Master left the shop by 8.00pm. Njideka became more apprehensive of the state of her husband when she received this report. Significantly too, none of Dan's business associates could be contacted at that time as their phones were all inaccessible. After feeding the household and having night prayers with them, Njide put the children to bed. Next, she drove out of the estate with the two apprentices to the nearby police station to report the case. Before she got home, Dan had arrived. He apologized and explained that he was busy negotiating business with some foreign partners. But Njide noticed the smell of alcohol and nicotine from his mouth; also, the competing and conflicting smells of perfumes oozing from his shirt and body.

A fortnight after, the pattern was repeated. One week after, the late night home coming surfaced again until it became a weekly affair. Njide stopped complaining because it earned her some thorough beating. She couldn't imagine what was happening to her marriage. She couldn't understand that her husband had suddenly changed. She had reported the matter to the two families but nobody had been able to bring a lasting solution to the crisis in her marriage. To think that Dan is unaware that Jide their first son is asthmatic is a danger sign of his negligence. Neither does he know that for two days running, his elderly mother is hospitalized with a case of stroke. Only time will reveal the rewards and regrets of Dan's reckless behaviour.

One early Saturday morning in April, the following year, Njideka's mobile phone rang while she was holding morning devotion with her household. After resisting to pick the phone for about three times, on the fourth call, Njide picked the call and heard a hoarse voice requesting her to come to the police station. Her husband was found earlier that day in his own car bleeding from his ear, nose and head. From this story, we discover that stubborn habits are consequential. These include,

a. Provokes Psychological distresses
b. Leads to loss of control over one's life.
c. Empowers dysfunctional lifestyle
d. Leads to economic wastage
e. Dangerous to others
f. Leads to unfulfilled dream
g. Leads to eternal doom

Let us consider these briefly.

Provokes Psychological Distresses: Stubborn habits promote psychological (mental and emotional) distresses both in the life of the victim and significant others. The distresses include anxiety, fear (phobia), guilt, self-condemnation and in some instances, alteration of one's state of consciousness. Also, the sense of judgement can be negatively and grossly affected. Of course, this is the foundation of most psychosomatic illnesses. Consider the high blood pressures, duedonal ulcers, nervous breakdowns and hypertensions. Our passion to a large extent, determines our level of health and progress in life. The strong drive to satisfy the craving of stubborn habits can create a conducive atmosphere for the onset or ascercabation of psychological and psychiatric illnesses. Nobody can thrive too long on the abnormally high release of adrenaline or testosterone. It is like living at the edge of a cliff. We all can climb to the cliff once in awhile but to make that place our abode will amount to courting destruction.

A second way stubborn habits endanger the human health is by breaking the immunity of the body and making it susceptible to diseases' attack. The continuous stretching and strainning of the body and mind through the activities of stubborn habits weakens the immune system. In order to compensate and complement what is lacking by over-activity, the cells, tissues and organs involved in the execution of stubborn habits, may experience

73

unusual growth (tumours). Poisoning of the system and other biochemical dysfunctions which may alter the healthy immune system are also possible outcomes.

Loss of Control

Engagement in stubborn habits is already an eloquent evidence of loss of control over one's life. Yet, there are deeper levels of enslavement and loses. Think of these examples;
- A stick of cigarette is controlling the decisions of an adult male.
- Less than a minute orgasm with a strange woman is the main motive why a responsible husband has become abusive to and negligent of his wife.
- Controlling an employee is the reason why a noble professional is pouring out poisonous words at the former.

Stubborn habits lead one to live like a victim. Instead of acting, you react; instead of being proactive you become a victim of circumstances.

Dysfunctional lifestyle

Stubborn habits represent dysfunctional lifestyles. Initially, one appears to be in control but not long after, that particular habit begins to control the individual. At this level, the individual neither thinks nor acts rationally. Irrationality and bestial instincts take over the life of the individual and the person is better described as a victim. Think of these examples,

- Why would a beautiful young lady endanger her life in the night seeking for a sex partner?
- Why would a young man covenant himself to suicide in order to kill people of another faith?
- Why would one prefer prison life to freedom?

The truth is that people with such negative lifestyles are already victims of dysfunctional mindsets.

Economic wastage

Stubborn habits create big holes in the purse. They are economically wasteful and destructive. For instance, marital violence is estimated to cost more than $5.8billion each year. Of this amount, $4.1 billion are for direct health care services and nearly $1.8billion are for the indirect costs of lost productivity or wages.[21] Imagine such huge sums thrown down the drain in order to satisfy an uncanny craving. Stubborn habits are like graves which can never be satisfied.

Dangerous to others

Stubborn habits endanger both the lives of the victim and others. Consider this example.

> On average, more than three women and one man are murdered by their intimate partners in this country every day. In 2000, 1,247 women were killed by their intimate partner. The same

---

[21] Centre of Disease Central and Prevention. Costs of Intimate Partner Violence Against Women.

year 440 men were killed by an intimate partner.[22]

Children also are an endangered species and likely the worst hit.

Studies suggest that 3.3 -10million children witness some form of domestic violence annually[23].

The dangers are not only physical. They are psychological, social, spiritual and economical. There are other forms of price which the relations, friends and communities which accommodate people with stubborn habits pay. I know a case of a lady who lost a pregnancy due to the constant nicotine she inhaled from her boss who was a chain smoker.

Unfulfilled Dreams

Someone rightly said that the road to hell is full of humans with good intentions. In the same manner, the graveyard is the richest part of the earth. The reason is obvious. The dreamers, visioners or heavily gifted couldn't pay the price of success. They allowed some enemy ambushments to cut down their dreams. Their energy and resources they should

[22] *Burea of Justice Statistics, Crime Data Brief. Intimate Partner Violence 1993) 2001, Feb 2003,*
[23] Carrison, Bonnie E. (1984) (Carrisoon, Bonnie E (1984), Children's Observations of Interpersonal Violence pp 147 -167) in A.R. Roberts (Eds) Battered women and their families (pp. 147-167) NY. Spinger, Straus MA (1992). Children as witnesses to mental violence: A risk factor for lifelong problems among Nationally representative sample of American men and women. Report of the Twenty-Third Ross Round Table. Columbus OH: Ross Laboratories.

have invested into creative ventures were wasted in gratifying the bestial desires of stubborn habits. For instance, the precious time and energy used to write this book would have been wasted in pursuing one of those bestial habits. Yet, the bell tolls for someone to turn over a new leaf.

Leads to Eternal Doom
No student remains in the school for ever. Every visitor to the market must return home at the appropriate time. So it is with this life. We shall all return home at the appropriate date. Death is a debt we all owe; but more than death, is our destination. Someone rightly said that each of us should live in such a way that when we die we shall be smiling in the celestial train while those we leave behind will be weeping. After all, when we were born, we were crying while everybody was joyful.

To err is human and to forgive is divine. Success and fulfillment in life involve obtaining divine mercy and forgiveness. Remaining victims of stubborn habits mean moving from the frying pan to the fire. It means spending eternity in doom. Each of us needs to meet men and women on their death beds. At such times, everybody tells the truth. No dying person gets engrossed in frivolity. No! They all desire to speak the truth. Those who lived well encourage their family members and friends to emulate them. Those who lived badly attempt to change as well as advice others to turn over a new leaf. They warn others to desist from evil. They even make confessions of their evil deeds, seek reconciliation and restitution. Evil habits, if not dealt with here can lead the individual to eternal doom.

Summary
Everyone can choose our actions but the consequences (in the wrong action) or reward (in the case of good action) is beyond our control. The consequences of indulging in stubborn habits are terrible. A deep reflection on this can help a victim to desire and plan to regain victory. May somebody have this reflection today and begin the journey to freedom.

Personal Reflection

1. In spite of the various degrees of consequences which emanate from involvement in stubborn habits, people tend to continue to indulge in them. What are the peculiar reasons that make people to become insensitive to these consequences?

_____

_____

2. Which of the consequences affect you most and why?

_____

_____

—

Chapter Nine

PRINCIPLES OF BREAKING STUBBORN HABITS

Emily, the mother of a toddler, has this habit of opening drawers and cupboards in the home but forgetting to close them back. Gab her accountant and meticulous husband has tried every method he knew to help Emily stop the habit, but all these attempts ended in futility. Gab resorted to verbal abuse when his initial efforts weren't yielding the expected result. Instead of solving the problem, it created more relationship problems between him and Emily.

Yet, Emily wouldn't change. Neither did Gab stop his nagging and verbal abuse against Emily. Then, he decided to attend a seminar on behavioural change. With gusto, he began to apply the principles of reward and punishment to extinguish Emily's irritating habit but these yielded little results. In fact, these conscious efforts made Emily to become tensed up each time they were together. On several occasions, both of them relapsed into their old patterns.

Remarkably one day Gab returned from work and found the house empty. A neighbour informed him that Emily and Karen their toddler girl were in the hospital due to wounds the girl sustained from a fall. Gab quickly drove to the hospital and when he found his wife and daughter, he further learnt that Karen's wound was worsened because she hit her face on the open mirror drawer of the master bedroom. Emily expected hell to break loose when they got home that day but surprisingly, Gab was calm. She was very sure that her husband was terribly hurt and would likely give her a show down but Gab never behaved as if anything was amiss. Rather, after a fortnight, during their usual outing and candle night date, he cuddled her and said, "Darling, from henceforth, I will neither scold nor nag you for keeping cupboards or drawers open in this house. I reached this agreement after the last incident.' Emily could neither believe her ears nor summon enough courage to look her husband in the eyes. She tried to control her heart from jumping out of her chest. Still holding her tightly, Gab continued, 'Of course, I have been through my own struggles. When I learnt of the circumstances of Karen's trauma, I was bitter. Later, I rejoiced and told myself that since your carelessness was responsible for her calamity, you will learn the bitter lesson to change. Though the change we expected is yet to come. Therefore, I made up my mind to release myself and you from this routine torment'.

Turning to face him now, Emily said, 'Really? Are you sure that you are no longer bitter? Really?' Facing her, Gab replied 'Yes I am no longer bitter. No doubt I was; had been but no more. Additionally, I permit you to keep any and every drawer in this house open. It is now my delight to close them". Like two teenagers newly in love, this couple began to dance. This, is my adaptation of a story I read in a marriage blog. We now consider some principles of breaking stubborn habits. First the list.

a. Accurate Assessment of the habit.
b. Determination to quit the habit
c. Focus on the Consequences.
d. Focus on the Rewards of Freedom
e. Be Accountable to someone.
f. Seek Professional help
g. Use creative Alternatives

We now consider each in more details.

Accurate Assessment
This is a foundational step to take. Socrates was credited with these words of wisdom that *an unexamined life is not worth living*. Therefore, anyone who sincerely desires to overcome any stubborn habit should begin with proper self evaluation in relation with such a habit. Ask some relevant questions like; "When did this habit begin? What circumstances or situations motivated the onset? What are the gains and loses, rewards and regrets of this habit? What degree of control does this habit have over me? Am I sincere in my desire to quit this habit? What is the cost of maintaining this stubborn habit?"

Furthermore, what form of restoration strategy would be best suited for the stubborn habit one is involved in? What pieces of information should be obtained? As tedious and challenging as these questions are, discovering them would enable the victim to make progress in solving the problem. It is like a case of *physician begin to heal yourself.* Would the physician cooperate?

A Resolute Determination to Quit the Habit
In most instances, a proper self evaluation will lead to one taking a resolute decision to quit the stubborn habit. The challenge is that most of the time, the victim may be limited in knowledge or be unable to raise deep questions on the subject matter. Such adequate assessments are normally carried out by psychologists, psychiatrists, counselors or doctors. This may be in the form of interview, questionnaire and more practically during counseling or psychotherapy sessions. I recall the case of a middle-aged chronic smoker who was battling with poverty, yet was helplessly wasting his meager resources in maintaining the smoking habit. In the process of clinical assessment, he discovered the huge economic wastage he was engaged in and the result was a resolute decision to quit.

Decision making belongs to the realm of the will, an important component of the mind or soul. It is difficult to succeed in any venture without exercising one's will power. Once one is able to align the will to a direction, both psycho-spiritual and biochemical forces combine to achieve the set target. Therefore, explore this power of the mind. Wield your will-power against the stubborn habit.

Decision making is a very important step in achieving success in life. As fearful and consequential as this step may look like, anyone who desires to achieve success must cultivate the attitude of being decisive in various aspects of life. We all need the courage to decide on a new course of action; whether to drop some habits or add a few others. May you rise up to the occasion and make the right decision today.

Focus on the Consequences
Every stubborn habit is consequential. We all face the deceptive notion that stubborn habits are beneficial. Not at all. If they have any benefits, such benefits are ephemeral and unfruitful. Consider the euphoria of vengeful anger or violent behaviour; the transient effervescence of drug addiction or sexual perversion. Added to these are the inestimable cost of maintaining these habits. These come in terms of physical and psychological, economic and emotional, social and spiritual dimensions.
Social stigmatization is one of the consequences of some anti-social stubborn habits. Take a case of paedophilia for an example. Paedophiles expose themselves to social ridicule and hatred.

Even if they turn over a new leaf, it may be difficult for some people in the community to receive them.

Focus on the Rewards of Freedom

Quitting a stubborn habit leads to enrichment of life in every sphere. I have observed the restoration of lives among drug addicts during the period of rehabilitation in the hospital, as well as observed others who failed to quit the habit. The elation and joy of achieving a new lease of life is normally unquantifiable.

Beginning with chemotherapy, the addict undergoes detoxication. As the poisonous chemicals in his system are neutralized and eliminated, the addict begins to experience renewal and restoration. Some of them who lost appetite for food will begin to eat normally as well as gain weight. Combining chemo- with psychotherapy will further boast the mental, emotional and physical health status of the patient. This positive turn of life events and possibilities should encourage victims of stubborn habits to quit the habit.

There is hope for recovery. There is opportunity to embrace change and become a champion rather than a victim.

Be Accountable to Someone

None of us is an island. Unfortunately, some people try to live a secluded or self-made life. The truth is that we become our best when we adopt a community and interdependent lifestyle.

Normally, there are three levels of human life – dependence, independence and interdependence[24]. At birth, we are totally dependent and this continues throughout our childhood stage. Then comes the adolescent period when we try to exercise our independence. Normally, most adolescents try to prove the point that they can take care of themselves but truly they cannot. In the third stage of life which is adulthood, we move to the highest and most fruitful level of human development – the interdependence stage.

However, every stage of the human life can benefit from interdependence which correlates with being accountable to someone. This is a formal arrangement whereby the victim of a stubborn habit seeks for help from someone he or she respects and requires that such one hold him or her accountable in the specific area of character challenge. By this arrangement, the victim reports regularly to the Accountable Partner on his or her failures and successes, trials, tests and testimonies in the battle against the stubborn habit. Also, liberty is given to the Accountable partner to ask questions, investigate further, intervene or even interrupt the activities of the victim in order to render assistance. I have been involved in such an Accountability relationship on several occasions. One of the prominent instances

---

[24] Stephen, R. Covey, *The 7 Habits of Highly Effective People*, UK, London: Simon & Schuster (1989)

was that of a married upcoming executive who had problem with Internet pornography. After reading a few of my books on the subject of overcoming sexual lust, he requested for this form of relationship. It did pay off well.

Accountability relationship can exist in different forms such as;
(a) Senior and junior mentoring format.
(b) Colleagues or equal partners
(c) Husband and wife
(d) A mentor and a group of mentees.

In our contemporary world of ever-increasing individualism and humanism, there exists a great need to engage the services of accountability partners. The awareness that one is responsible to another whom he gives account of his activities can even act as a deterrent to engaging in the misdemeanour. Again, a problem shared is a problem half-solved. There are some of us who by the virtue of our position or status as bosses or heads of organizations, report to nobody. It can be a dangerous scenario causing one to misuse it and become narcissistic, delutional or even dictatorial. Truly it is disadvantageous to live without an adviser. Any human who has nobody to provide occasional correction, query or even rebuke may not be far away from trouble. In the same manner, we all need encouragement, support and admiration on our road to success in life. An accountability relationship will fulfil all these responsibilities.

Seek Professional Help

Often, we human beings think and behave as if we are omniscient. We assume we know everything. Next, we develop short-cuts to every problem. Fast foods, cars, marriage, growth, medication and also a consequent fast death follows. Daily, the standard of living follows a downward trend of degeneration and depletion. Many in our generation tend to detest professionalism and standardization. Ours has become *a generation of anything goes*. Imagine the havoc of self-medication; the great damage of examination malpractices; the inestimable devastation of unqualified teachers, quack pharmacists or doctors etc.

Therefore, victims of stubborn habits should seek professional help. Refrain from *self-medication* or patronizing quacks. Relevant professional helpers include;

Medical doctors – who are specialists in dealing with physical and physiological health problems.

Psychologists – who are specialists in handling emotional and mental health problems.

Psychiatrists – who use both chemo and psychotherapies to handle psychological problems.

Counselors – who use some psychological principles to handle behaviour problems.

Spiritual leaders – who use godly principles to help those in diverse problems.

Use Creative Alternative

The time, energy and resources invested into perpetrating evil can be invested into positive and productive ventures. Personally, I find this approach very effective and useful. It is one veritable strategy I use to deal with the temptation of lust. At such occasions of temptation, I divert my interest into some creative activities like, reading an inspirational literature, writing or watching an educative film.

As we can see, this strategy will work more effectively with the assistance of others like exercise of personal discipline, focus on the rewards of freedom and taking a resolute decision.

It is important that the creative activities you adopt be the types that are relevant and of interest to you. Also, ensure that they aren't linking bridges to the stubborn habit. Note that initially, you will experience some resistance and difficulty but keep at it. Like it is said, the journey of a thousand miles begins with a step in the right direction. Therefore, begin.

Summary

Only a few mortals are aware of the immense capacity they possess. The resources wasted in the satisfaction of stubborn habits can be reinvested into the pursuit of a noble lifestyle. The mind can be so enlightened and empowered that the evil roots of stubborn habits are destroyed and a new foundation laid for successful living.

Personal Reflection

1. What new principle(s) of breaking stubborn habits have I learnt from the chapter?

   _____

   _____

   _____

2. What practical step(s) can I take to make the new lesson(s) a reality?
   a. _____
   b. _____
   c. _____

3. Which of these principles of breaking stubborn habits is most relevant to me and why?

   _____

   _____

   _____

Chapter Ten

THE SPIRITUAL APPROACH

Facts are stubborn. Truths are sacred. Try as some of us may, we may not be able to change the truth. Trying to change the truth is comparable to using bare hands to drive a six foot nail into a rock. For instance, the human personality is tripartite, made up of body, soul and spirit. Over the years, humanity has tried to distort or deny this truth. There is the dualism theory which postulates that mortals are made up of matter and spirit. There is the Freudian psychoanalytic theory that states that the human mind is made up of *Id, Ego* and S*uperego.* This view is even closer to the tripartite theory of body, soul (mind) and spirit. Others believe that *Homo sapiens* are predominantly made up of matter.

However, whichever view one holds, my stand is that human beings are tripartite. We are spirits who are endowed with a mind and live in a body. Our subject matter, the development of habits affects the three components of the human personality. How? The voice of the body is emotion; the voice of the mind (or soul) is reason while the voice of the spirit is faith. Every human being experiences these three levels of life as well as manifests these three expressions. Habit formation and termination go beyond biochemistry, and reaches to the psycho-spiritual realm. Consider this diagramme.

The Tripartite Nature of Mortals

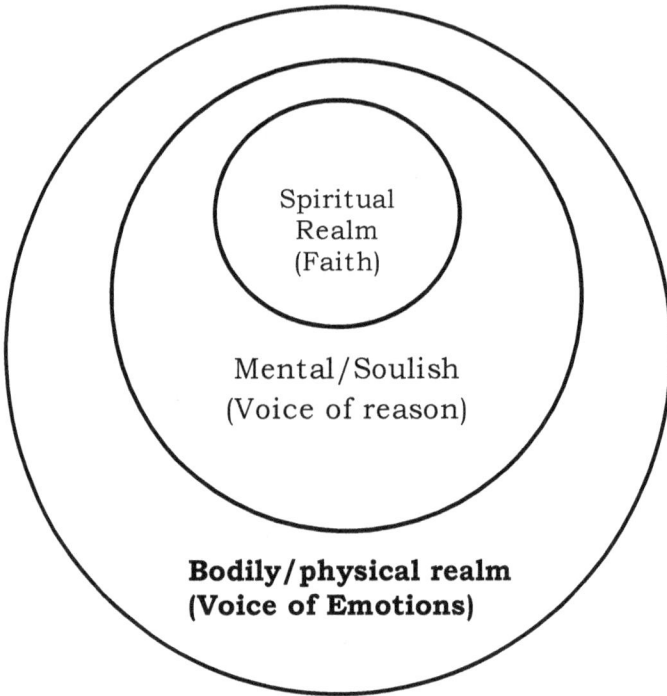

Spiritual
Realm
(Faith)

Mental/Soulish
(Voice of reason)

**Bodily/physical realm
(Voice of Emotions)**

No patient gets healed without an expression of faith in the doctor, type of therapy or both. In the same manner, no patient experiences divine healing without an express faith (or belief) that such a positive change or turnaround is possible. The value of faith can be further enunciated by considering the consequences of its absence. Imagine, a marriage relationship fraught with mistrust, a business partnership conducted on the basis of prejudice, a learning relationship executed with prejudice. Without faith (belief, expression of confidence in someone, thing, or event) life on earth will be an impossible task.

Beyond expression of faith in the expertise, character or gift of our fellow mortals, there is need to express our personal confidence in the Supernatural Being (God). This form of expression of confidence is necessary to terminate stubborn habits for specific reasons. First, it completes and complements the efforts of the other two human components of the body and mind. Again, it empowers the human personality to deal with strange evil forces. Beyond the caricature references of the unintelligent crowd to the forces of darkness as the cause of human tragedy, there are several significant manifestations of evil in our lives and society which authenticate the reality of an organized evil kingdom that is governed by evil personalities. A few instances can suffice. Scientific psychology and psychiatry alone cannot explain why a youth can take up a gun, and without provocation, kill several of his mates and colleagues in school. Neither can we explain how some psychotic problems are beyond remedy; why some psychiatric cases are terminal; nor how several mysterious occurrences begin and degenerate beyond our scientific managerial ability.

In 2012, I was in Berlin Germany and encountered a young teenage Chinese girl who was confined to a rehabilitation centre. The problem began with the girl's excessive love to watch bizarre cartoon programmes. Next, she began to develop interest in watching horror films such as vampire, witchcraft and their likes. Then, she became phobic and began to detest the sight of her medical doctor parents. She could still tolerate seeing her father, but not her mother. She stopped going to school and church and would rather stay in her room. At this stage, the parents had to take her to a rehabilitation centre. It was from the Rehab that her father brought her to see me. The day I met her, I could only pray from a distance because she was apprehensive; in fact she ran away from me and her father who brought her. Quickly the father and I ran after her while I continued to exorcise the evil spirits who were tormenting her. Later, she was returned to the rehabilitation centre and in less than a fortnight, she had made appreciable progress.

My thinking is that this case had both psychological and spiritual roots and as well needed both approaches of treatment. I sense that many cases of stubborn habits are in this mould.

Most often, the spiritual realm controls the mental and emotional while these two control the physical. This is the ideal; but the real, may differ from this arrangement. Yet, the connection between these three realms cannot be denied. Consider these following diagrammes showing the control of life events.

Diagramme Showing Control of Life Events.

a. **Realm I** (Indisciplined Below Average Personality)

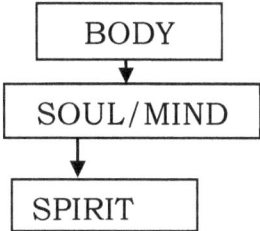

```
┌──────────────┐
│     BODY     │
└──────────────┘
       │
       ▼
┌──────────────┐
│  SOUL/MIND   │
└──────────────┘
       │
       ▼
┌──────────────┐
│    SPIRIT    │
└──────────────┘
```

b. **Realm II** (Mediocre)

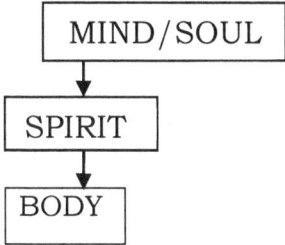

```
┌──────────────┐
│  MIND/SOUL   │
└──────────────┘
       │
       ▼
┌──────────────┐
│    SPIRIT    │
└──────────────┘
       │
       ▼
┌──────────────┐
│     BODY     │
└──────────────┘
```

c. **Ideal** – Disciplined and Successful Personality.

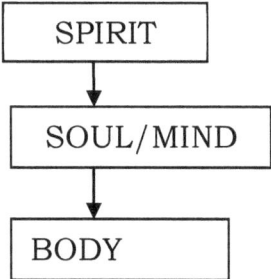

```
┌──────────────┐
│    SPIRIT    │
└──────────────┘
       │
       ▼
┌──────────────┐
│  SOUL/MIND   │
└──────────────┘
       │
       ▼
┌──────────────┐
│     BODY     │
└──────────────┘
```

NB: The arrows in the three diagrammes show the direction of control.

Deep calls to deep just as shallowness beckons to shallowness. The spirit of man (spirit-man or innermost man) is the deepest part of the human personality. Every habit or attitude is empowered from this depth of the human spirit. Like the body, it has its own spiritual senses. The three components of the body, mind and spirit are intertwined and interspaced. This is a major reason why when one part is assailed, it significantly affects the others. As we have physical senses of sight (eye), hearing (ear), touch (skin), speech (tongue) and smell (nose), there exist also the mental and spiritual counterparts. Consider the following instances:

a. The activities of the dream state. The physical lies motionless on a bed while the mind and spirit utilizing all the senses are active.
b. The meditation experience in our state of wakefulness. One can sit down in a place and yet the mind and spirit perform all the activities of the physical body without exhibiting any bodily movement,
c. The example of the woman with twelve years' issue of blood. Inspite of the fact that multitudes were touching Jesus, and reported no spectacular experience, this Gentile woman, empowered by the force of the inner voice and conviction *(she said within herself)*, touched the Messiah first

with the hand of her spirit, then her mind and lastly, her body. She was instantly healed.[25]
d. The reality of silent discussion and thinking process. Right inside our minds we perform all the activities of the physical body.

Let us consider some spiritual steps that enable the breaking of stubborn habits. These include;

a. Repentance
b. Adequate Spiritual Diet
c. Restitution
d. Fasting
e. Personal Devotion
f. Engage in Service.
g. Engage in love revolution

Repentance
By every means, this term is a positive one. It is like undergoing an operation in order to remove an inflamed or infected appendix. Repentance is an indication that one is on the pathway of recovery. In Greek, repentance is referred to as *mentanoia*; which means, a change of heart which manifests in a new set of behaviours and speech. It begins with self-examination and acceptance that one is wrong. Furthermore, it involves accepting that God is right. His word is correct and we are in the wrong. It means accepting that one's engagement in stubborn

---
[25] Mk. 5:25-34

habit is harmful and shameful. It involves accepting responsibility for one's actions and errors. It means ending the despicable game of buck-passing.

For I acknowledge my transgressions: and my sin is ever before me. Against thee, thee only have I sinned and done this evil in thy sight.[26]

This was the inspired words of David, the musician and warrior, lion-killer king of Israel who committed both adultery and murder in order to covet another man's wife. When he realized his grievous error, he had a positive change of mind. He acknowledged the shamefulness of his actions and behaviour. Next, he sought for forgiveness.

One may rationalize and believe that one's involvement in stubborn habit neither harms nor endangers anybody. But it is false. Engagement in any negative behaviour and moreso habit, is consequential to both the individual and others. An African proverb says that *when one finger touches oil, it spreads to the others.* Another says that *when the eyes begin to weep, the noses cannot but join the mourning team.* Mankind may never succeed in wiping out entirely the idea of communal living. Like we noted earlier, the highest level of human relationship is interdependence. The idea is that we are creatures of value and can only be at our best

---

[26] Ps. 61:3-4

when we operate as generous givers as well as grateful receivers. As mortals, we are neither indispensable nor useless. We all need each other to succeed.

Repentance also involves making a decision to turn away from the stubborn habit. It includes, confession of the error to God.

> *If we confess our sins, he is faithful and just to forgive us our sins, and to cleanse us from all unrighteousness.*[27]

Finally, repentance involves accepting forgiveness. It is exchanging our filth and dirt with God's forgiveness and mercy. It is like taking a bath in a clean stream. It is receiving our once dirty dresses from a good dry cleaner. This makes sense as we know that to err is human while to forgive is divine. Will you take this step?

Ingest Adequate Spiritual Diet
We are as healthy and strong as our diet. Poor or unbalanced diet leads to poor or ill health. On the other hand, a healthy and balanced diet promotes good health.
This principle applies to the health of the body, mind and spirit. We are what we feed on. Therefore, our bodies need a physical balanced diet, our minds, mentally rich and challenging diet of literature. In

---

[27] 1Jn.1:9

the same manner, our spirits or innermost beings need inspirational and divine messages to live and prosper. No spiritual food is more qualified to feed our spirit than the Word of God; because it is inspired. 'All scripture is given by inspiration of God, and is profitable for doctrine, for reproof, for correction, for instruction in righteousness'.[28]

The word of God (written, spoken or illustrated) is provided for the benefit and blessings of human beings. It is provided to teach, correct and instruct human beings on the excellent pathways of life. Just like the spirit or innermost part of our being, the word of God is divine and eternal. Remarkably, these two will be the only survivors in eternity. Every other creature we can access with our five senses (sight, smell, touch, hearing and thirst) will perish on this earth. Take note of this revelation.

---

[28] 2Tim.3:16

Accurate Dietary Requirements of a Triparitite Being

Number	Human component	Diet	Purpose
i	Body (Physical)	Physical Food (Carbohydrates, Protein, Vitamins, Minerals)	Healthy and Strong Body
ii	Soul/Mind (Psychological Mental & Emotional)	Academic and mentally challenging materials.	Sound and Creative Mind
iii	Spirit (Spiritual)	Inspirational materials (written, spoken, acted, etc.)	Healthy and Powerful Spirit.

Note the types of personalities that can emerge from this matrix:

a. One with a healthy body, and mind but dead spirit.
b. One with a healthy body, sick mind and dead spirit.
c. One with a sick body, healthy mind and spirit.
d. One with a sick body and mind and dead spirit.
e. One with a healthy body, mind and spirit.
f. One with a sick body, healthy mind and dead spirit.
g. One with sick body, sick mind and healthy spirit.

h. One with healthy body, mine and spirit.

Consider the level of disadvantage and distress physical and mental sicknesses create. That of spiritual sickness may not be initially obvious, but it produces the worst consequences. Spiritual sickness is rooted in poor or negligence of spiritual diet. Of course, the spirit needs to be regenerated (given life) through repentance because corpses don't (and cannot) eat.

> *Wherefore laying aside all malice, and all guile, and hypocrisies, and envies, and all evil speaking;*
>
> *As newborn babes, desire the sincere milk of the word, that ye may grow thereby.[29]*

Milk represents balanced diet for children. However, no adult survives on milk. Children begin with milk and as they grow older, they begin to add solid food materials to their meals. In the same manner, growing spiritual children need to add solid spiritual food items to the initial diet. What constitutes spiritual milk and meat?

The spiritual milk refers to the scriptures which concentrate on the blessings and benefits of the New life

---

[29] 1Pet. 2:1-2

The solid meals and meat refer to scriptures that require us to be responsible children of God. We have to relate with both privileges and responsibilities.

> For when for the time ye ought to be teachers, ye need that one teach you again which be the first principles of the oracles of God; and are become such as have need of milk, and not of strong meat. For every one that useth milk is unskilled in the word of righteousness: for he is a babe.

> But strong meat belongeth to them that are full age, even those who by reason of use have their senses exercised to discern both good and evil.[30]

There are various levels of interaction with the word of God. These include, reading, studying, memorizing, meditation, praying, speaking and acting on it. All these steps are useful in dealing with stubborn habits. The word of God in our minds and spirits help us to overcome stubborn habits in some specific ways such as;

i. Acting as a defensive weapon against temptations. On several occasions, it has enabled me to overcome mental lust. On one

---

[30] Hebs. 5:12-14

cold night in a lonely hotel during a trip abroad and under intense temptation to become indiscreet with television remote, the word rose up from my heart as a defence.

Know ye not that they which run in a race run all, but one receiveth the prize? So run, that ye may obtain. And every man that striveth for the mastery is temperate in all things. Now they do it to obtain a corrupt crown: but we an incorruptible. I therefore so run, not as uncertainly so fight I, not as one that beateth the air: But I keep under my body, and bring into subjection: lest that by any means, when I have preached to others, I myself should be a castaway.[31]

It was efficacious. I surrendered the remote. I know the frustrating effect of defeat as well as the joy of victory over stubborn habit. That night I celebrated. I felt so light and joyful. The word was my defence.

ii. The word can act as an offensive weapon against stubborn habits. As you renew your mind with the word, it fills your mind and heart and acts as a spiritual disinfectant to both destroy existing spiritual germs as well as

---

[31] 1Cor. 9:24-27

prevent further invasion. This is why temptation and exposure to stimulus of the stubborn habit can no longer produce corresponding response. "Surely in vain, the net as spread in the sight of any bird'.[32]

iii. The word acts as balanced and sumptuous meat for the spirit being. Consequently, it doesn't allow space for garbage. Let the word of God dwell in your heart richly.[33] Now go and begin to feed your spirit-being on the inspired word of God.

Obtain Personal Freedom

Stubborn habit can be as a result of spiritual bondage. C.S. Lewis captures the balanced sense of this matter when he said,

There are two equal and opposite errors into which our race can fall about the devils. One is to disbelieve in their existence. The other is to believe, and to feel an extensive and unhealthy interest in them.[34]

The existence of evil activities of demons or devils are obvious. Yet, these don't erase the fact about human responsibility. The devil and his demons tempt, lure, try to deceive, allure but the decision to act still lies

---

[32] Prov.1:17
[33] Col. 3:16
[34] C.S. Lewis, The Screw Tape Letters, San Francisco: Harper Collins Edition (2001).

with the human person. Even in an extreme case of demonic activity like possession, the human person isn't totally incapable of resisting the enemy.

Demonic activities in the lives of people operate at various levels as:

- Oppression – represents various forms of demonic attacks and offences from outside the individual's life.

- Obsession – Demonic activity that results in the preoccupation of the mind with evil or wicked thoughts, or negatively fixed ideas. Examples include, suicidal thoughts, rape, bitterness et cetera.

- Possession – Refers to a case whereby the evil spirit indwells a human person, animal or environment. The indwelling can be in the body, mind or spirit or all. This is the worst kind of demonic activity. There was a case of an undergraduate in a Nigerian University who locked himself up at home and refused to return to school. Infact, the case was so bad that he could defecate in his room and was no longer mindful of personal hygiene. He caused his father much trauma and pain. The man was ready to pay all the bills but his son was neither ready to live decent nor return to school. By the time we visited, the boy was very uncooperative. We recommended that the man engaged the service of a psychiatric hospital.

Prayer for release from stubborn habits is referred to as deliverance or exorcism. It can be effective but, it is better to combine this with behavioural change strategies. One of the reasons why there exist a high level of recidivism among demon-possessed or obsessed people is negligence of behavioural change approach. The demon may go but the conditioned response is unaffected. Just like the nerves, arteries and muscles of the body get conditioned to some stimuli and therefore respond in specific ways, so do the cells of the brain. A personal example may suffice here. I am used to bathing with cold water. But on one occasion, I used an electric kettle in our bedroom to boil hot water. However, I stepped into the bathroom and had the usual cold bath. I was half-way through when I realized that I didn't use the hot water I boiled. This is a typical case of conditioned response or habitual behaviour empowered by the conditioning of brain cells.

In using this spiritual strategy, try and avoid the use of quacks. Some people have endangered their lives by inviting wrong spiritual authority. Be careful with the choice of deliverance ministers or spiritual healers. Yet, the fake doesn't nullify the role of the genuine.

Practice Restitution

As little as this phrase is, 'I am sorry", its effect is significantly therapeutic. Some offences or errors are committed against God and while others are against our fellow mortals. Therefore, after obtaining forgiveness from God, the offender needs to equally make peace with mortals.

'Confess your faults one to another, and pray one for another, that ye may be healed.'[35]

Acknowledging our errors and seeking for forgiveness brings healing and restoration on both sides of the relationship – offender and offended. The liar, kleptomaniac, drunkard, drug addict, spouse abuser, rapist, murderer, witch, wizard and other habitual offenders, all need to confront their evil habits and seek for the forgiveness of those they offended.

Yet, restitution can go beyond confession and verbal assent of wrong doing. Basically, restitution represents all attempts to repair what was destroyed. Therefore, it will include repayment of debts or returning of stolen property, and rebuilding of broken bridges. In difficult and extreme cases like murder, the offender should seek counsel. Such cases need caution and the input of spiritual and legal advisers.

Engage in Fasting

---

[35] James 5:16

Fasting deals with self-denial of not only foods and drinks but also other legitimate comforts of life so that one can give more attention and concentration to spiritual issues. Fasting repositions one to gain access to blessings. Fasting changes mortals but not God. Fasting is a significant means of demonstrating one's seriousness to obtain a request.

Fasting can be specific (for a period of time or to obtain a need) or regular. In the case of dealing with stubborn habit, both strategies are useful because it involves the exchange of physical energy with the spiritual. In this way, fasting is transformational. During fasting, one should be seriously engaged in spiritual exercises such as repentance, meditation, prayer, and study of scriptures.

During my undergraduate years, I had a friend who used the power of fasting to deal with sexual lust. Infact he was so serious that sometimes, he would go for three days without eating. Of course, he drank water. He had positive result. This is consistent with the scripture which says,

> Is this not the fast that I have chosen. To loose the bonds of wickedness, to undo the heavy burdens, to let the oppressed go free, And that you break every yoke?[36]

---

[36] Isaiah 58:6

Yet fasting or abstinence is more effective when it is supported with prayer and the study of scriptures. Denying oneself of food and drink or any other need without engaging in prayer and the study of the word of God is equivalent to starving. Consequently, the quality of a fasting programme is predicated on the quality of spiritual exercise one engages in during the fast.

In practical terms, one can abstain from engaging in any activity or event which lures one back to the stubborn habit. *Abstain from all appearance of evil.*[37] Some other times, the appearance of evil may be a location, venue or even human association. Wisdom demands that one exercises self-control or restraint from such tempting events.

Engage in Personal Devotion
We are as strong as our devotional commitment. Weak devotional life produces weak spirituality and vice versa. Early in my Christian life, I learnt a few principles that are still useful today. First, we were taught that, *no Bible reading, no breakfast.* This slogan made spiritual food a priority over physical food. Again, we learnt that, we should give God the first waking period of our lives by praying and studying our Bibles early in the morning. The third relevant lesson here is that we should pay a tithe of our financial earning and also of our time daily to

---

[37] 1Thess. 5:22

God.   Literally, this means spending at least one hundred and forty four minutes (2 hours 24 minutes) in personal devotion.

These are simple but profound strategies that will help one to remain spiritually healthy and strong. It will equally occupy one's energy and time so that little or nothing will be left for frivolity.

Personal devotion should be a regular spiritual exercise.   It should be a desirable daily business which provides divine direction as well as inoculate one against the forces of temptation.   One has to create time and venue for such a daily crucial meeting with God.   It can, and has always been a turning point for many.

The use of Devotional Books can be a good beginning point but don't stop there. Try to go beyond this and stretch your spirit and mind.   The more of inspirational literature you consume, the better your thought and emotional life. Now get busy.

Be Diligent in Service
Truly, an idle mind is the devil's workshop. Work, particularly the good and noble type, frustrates evil. Like someone rightly said, evil triumphs when noble men keep quiet. And I add that evil triumphs when noble men cherish idleness.

Note that the time, energy and resources wasted in the execution of stubborn habit can be utilized to create a holy, harmonious, healthy haven here for self and others.

Service is best executed from our area of ability or gifting. Each of us has at least one area of interest or passion which when discovered, developed and deployed, will both enhance our lives as well help many others to succeed in life. Please locate yours. It may be a physical, mental or spiritual service. Get busy with service and work but avoid becoming a workaholic. Try to draw a balance between work and rest.

Effective service or work is targeted at meeting peculiar needs, solving particular problems or adding value to lives. In other words, our work should be productive and not be one of just being busy.

> Go to the ant, you sluggard! Consider her ways and be wise, which having no captain, overseer or ruler, provides her supplies in the summer, and gathers her food in the harvest. How long will you slumber, O sluggard? When will you rise from your sleep?[38]

The lesson of diligent productivity from the ants is instructive. Now go and do same.

Engage in Love Revolution

---

[38] Prov.6:6,7

Love remains the strongest positive emotion on earth and eternity. Think of the genuine love between a newly married couple. Recall the high degree of affection, affirmation and affiliation between this couple.

I

Love Revolution

No sacrifice is too dear
No gift is priceless
No danger is threatening enough
To quench the flame of love

II

Barriers and barricades
Obstacles and oppositions
Like paper tigers crumble
In the face of genuine love

III

Love like shepherd boy David dares
Like an ocean it accommodates
As a conflagration it conquers
Till it consummates and consolidates.

IV

Like an armed warrior
Decisive, determined and daring
Acquire sophisticated armour
To begin a new Revolution.

V

Like a lovestroke damsel
Restless and yet restful

The Bride of Christ
Engage in a sacrificial Love Revolution.

Stubborn habit can be conquered by engaging in love revolution. At present, a victim of stubborn habit is love struck with the wrong subject – the stubborn habit. What is needed is a change of love subject. Exchange the love (lust) expressed towards the stubborn habit with love for Jesus. Divorce the stubborn habit and marry Jesus Christ. Why?

A basic reason for this radical decision is because Jesus Christ is the only true Love available to mankind. God is love[39]. Again, He first loved us by sacrificing His life for us. We need to reciprocate this divine outpouring of love by surrendering our lives to, as well as living for Him.

Living without Jesus Christ as our Lord and Saviour is the worst crime mankind will ever engage in. It is the life of an eternally doomed law-breaker.

Reciprocating the love of God by surrendering our lives to Jesus is the beginning of love revolution. We must continue in this love of God until we become filled with the Holy Spirit. This love revolution must grow into a daily lifestyle of sincere worship.

But the hour is coming and now is, when the true worshippers will worship the Father in

---
[39] 1John 3:9

Spirit and truth; for the Father is seeking such to worship Him. God is a Spirit, and those who worship Him must worship Him in Spirit and truth.[40]

The call to engage in love revolution is a call to enjoy intimacy with God. It goes beyond obtaining new life in Christ. It is the deeper walk with God. It is falling in love with AGAPE (God) because God is love[41]. It is being filled with the Spirit and yielding totally unto Him. 'And do not be drunk with wine, in which is dissipation; but be filled with the Spirit."[42]

Beloved, God is calling us to be intoxicated with His love. He wants us to be charged and charmed, filled to the brim as well as be formed by divine love. Consider this great hymn.

The Wondrous Cross
When I survey the wondrous cross
On which the Prince of glory died,
My richest gain I count but loss,
And pour contempt on all my pride.

Forbid it, Lord that I should boast,
Save in the death of Christ my God!
All the vain things that charm me most,
I sacrifice them to His blood.

---

[40] John 4:23,24

[41] 1John 4:18

[42] Ephesians 5:18

115

See from His head, His hands, His feet,
Sorrow and love flow mingled down!
Did ever such love and sorrow meet,
Or thorns compose so rich a crown?

Were the whole realm of nature mine,
That were a present far too small;
Love so amazing, so divine,
Demands my soul, my life, my all![43]

Isaac Watts, is the Author of this timeless hymn. The hymn is based on the Galatians passage that says, "But God forbid that I should glory, save in the cross of our Lord Jesus Christ, by whom the world is crucified unto me, and I unto the world."[44]

One authority has it that,

> *Watt's lifelong ambition, according to his own words, was to be a servant to churches and a helper of Christians. The majestic phrases of this deeply hymn are as moving today as when Watts penned it in 1707. The hymn has been set to more than one time but perhaps the most popular is that of Edward Miller, who wrote his music in 1790, some forty-two years after Watts' death.[45]*

---

[43] Library timeless truths.org/music (Accessed January 24 2017)
[44] Galatians 6:14
[45] The Story Behind... When I survey The Wonderous Cross. www.plymonthbrethren.org/article (Accessed January 24, 2017)

Watts represents so many saints of God who are sold out to God's will and love. Their pursuit and purpose is to gain Christ and not necessarily His blessings. Abraham experienced this love revolution for God and forsook all to answer the call of God. Joseph's love for God was so significant that the former in spite of constant and pleasurable seductive temptation, refused to surrender. How could he do such evil against God by committing fornication? Joseph declared. Peter struck by this same love, abandoned his lucrative fishing business at the highest point of business success. Paul gave up his religious, social and political privileges to pursue this love of God through Christ Jesus.

Mary Magdalene, a notorious prostitute renounced all her evil ways and wholeheartedly surrendered to the love of the Saviour. Even when other disciples abandoned Jesus, Mary was the only one standing and waiting to see Him. The Lord rewarded her by giving her the privilege of appearing to her first and committing the Gospel of His resurrection to her. Each of us can grow into the likeness of God's image and love Him with all our hearts. The result will be that the love for stubborn habits will wane and become totally extinguished. Let us rise up to this. *Love so amazing, so divine demands our souls, our lives, our all.*

Summary

Enjoying sound health is priceless. In the same way, freedom is one of the best gifts a mortal can enjoy.

Consequently, every noble effort geared towards obtaining freedom is worthwhile. Humanity will always reap immeasurable benefits by harnessing godly principles which will enable her to rule over evil forces. All deliberate efforts to bring God into personal battles will yield immense dividends. May we realize our great need for Divinity and also seek for divine help.

Personal Reflection

1. What aspect of this chapter on the Spiritual Approach to overcoming stubborn habits resonates with you and why?

   _____

   _____

   _____

2. Using these spiritual principles, how can you move from your present (real) condition to the desired (ideal)?

   _____

   _____

   _____

3. In your own understanding, what does it mean to fall in love with Jesus Christ?

_____

_____

_____

Chapter Eleven

PRACTICAL STEPS FOR BREAKING STUBBORN HABITS

The two signs of middle age among many males namely: greying of hairs and development of pot-belly were already evident in Kevin's (pseudonym) life. Once a lanky and handsome man, the latter sign was a huge threat to Kevin's life. He was comfortable with the strategies of engaging in regular exercise and eating balanced diet, but found it extremely difficult to avoid late night dinner. When Kevin discovered that all his efforts to regain his youthful shape was aborted by his inability to eat early dinner, he decided to tackle the issue headlong.

Consequently, Kevin obtained the assistance of Juan, his wife, to help him to eat early dinner. The first few days of the exercise were traumatic. Juan, a disciplinarian, ensured that Kevin's order was carried out to the letter. She supplied his dinner as a take away pack and gave it to the driver to deliver. Kevin normally ate lunch in the company's restaurant with other senior staff and used the takeaway pack from home for dinner at 6pm or 7pm. This plan was reliable and efficient until....

The real challenge Kevin faced began on the first day of the programme when he arrived home between 8:30-9pm. After listening to the evening news, Kevin would be hungry again around 10pm and would desire to eat. Normally, the craving for food would increase to a very high degree and Kevin would begin to request Juan to provide the former with some food items. Initially, the latter would be quiet and pretend to be ignorant of the husband's action until the matter became unbearable. When Kevin begins to approach the kitchen or fridge to actualize his goal of getting food to eat, Juan would rise up to stop him. It is normally a dramatic scenario. "Honey, you don't understand what I am going through", Kevin would declare. Immediately, Juan would hold her husband's hands, embrace and slowly turn him around singing "My sweetheart is a winner always".

This story relates with the focus of this chapter which considers the practical steps to breaking stubborn habits. These would include,
a. Understanding the root
b. A growing detest
c. Practicing delayed gratification
d. Employing mind control mechanisms
e. Engaging in systematic desensitization

Diagrammatically, these practical steps will look like this;

e	Engage in Systematic Desensitisation
d	Employ Mind Control
c	Practice Delayed Gratification
b	Develop a Growing Detest
a	Understand the Root of Stubborn Habits

NB: *Arrowing showing the stages of the practical steps for breaking stubborn habits.*

Understanding the Roots of stubborn Habits

I once sent a mail to a friend's email box but it was rejected. Later, I discovered that the reason for the failure of my posted mail was because I did not add the full stop in his email. As small as this error was, it frustrated all my noble efforts. This error was the root of my failure and frustration.

Therefore, the practical beginning point to handle stubborn habits is to understand the root or foundation. Stubborn habits are the offsprings of evil desires. This is a psychological root. It involves both mental and emotional aspects of life.

> *And remember, no one who wants to do wrong should ever say, "God is tempting me". God is never tempted to do wrong and he never tempts anyone else either. Temptation comes from the lure of our own evil desires. These evil desires lead to evil actions and evil actions lead to death".*
> Please note the sequence of events.[46]

Evil desire leads to evil action which eventually leads to death.

---

[46] James 1:13-14 NLT

A successful onslaught against stubborn habits would involve avoiding engaging in such negative habits such as:

a. Passing buck
b. Engaging in blame game
c. Denial of personal responsibilities
d. Hypocrisy/Lying
e. Ignorance

In other words, one who is truly interested in overcoming any stubborn habit should begin by understanding and acknowledging their central personal role in engaging in such a habit. It is a matter of personal choice.

No doubt every mortal has a proclivity towards one evil desire or the other.

> *When you follow the desires of sinful nature, your lives will produce these evil results: sexual immorality, impure thoughts, eagerness for lustful pleasure, idolatry, participation in demonic activities, hostility, quarrelling, jealousy, outbursts of anger , selfish ambitions, the feeling that everyone is wrong except those in your own little group, envy, drunkenness, wild parties and other kinds of sin. Let me tell you again, as I*

have before, that anyone living that sort of
life will not inherit the kingdom of God.[47]

While every mortal has a natural inclination towards engaging in one or the other of these stubborn habits which are rooted in evil desires, we all have an immense capacity to overcome them. The energy and resources invested into engaging in them can be reversed and invested into creative and noble habits,

The second arm of the root of stubborn habit is demonic. Jesus' answer to His Jewish brethren who claimed to be the true stock of Abraham highlights this view. We read thus,

Ye are of your father the devil, and the lusts
of your father ye want to do.[48]

Satan is the author of lusts (evil desires). He is the manufacturer and marketer of evil desires. He is the advertiser and advocate of evil desires. Therefore, when the peculiar evil proclivity of any mortal combines with this satanic allurement, it produces evil actions which may graduate into stubborn habits.

An appropriate African proverb on this occasion is that *the rat inside informed the one outside that there is fish in grandmother's basket.* The human evil

---

[47] Gal. 5:19-21 NLT

[48] Jn. 8:44 KJV

desire is the inside partner of the satanic outside evil desire. This understanding is necessary to overcome the arsenal of stubborn habits.

A growing Detest Against Stubborn Habits

Knowledge is power. It enhances our choices, empowers the will as well as enlightens us on our path to success.

In the same vein, proper knowledge of stubborn habits will enable the victim to be an overcomer. Understanding the roots, the potency and consequences of stubborn habits will create a deep detest for engaging in them. Examples of this phenomenon include the following:

a. When I learnt of the damage of alcoholism to my heart (particularly, my liver), I resolved to stop drinking.
b. As an adult, when I discovered the health hazards of sugar consumption, I began to regulate my consumption level of soft drinks.
c. As a product of a polygamous home, who witnessed the high premium of one man marrying more than one wife, I began early to fight against promiscuity in my life.
d. One of my paternal uncles was seriously involved with occult practices. Of course, he obtained much wealth and social influence but he died a miserable death and worse still, his house became a dung hill barely two years after his death. I

swore to have nothing to do with any form of occult practice.

These four examples point to the fact that a careful observation and understanding of the consequences of stubborn habits produces a growing detest for indulging in them.

Genuine, deep and sustained agitation is needed for one to be liberated from the trials and troubles of stubborn habits.

Like a baby tied to a mother's back
Unlike a mother, stubborn habit
As a murderer, hooks the neck
Like a blood-sucking hookworm assails its victim
As a monstrous predator
Inflamed with murderous intent
Unhindered and undeterred
Attempts to harass
Longs to lure and limit
But agitation and angst
Revulsion and revolution
Boiling to a hilt
Pours out torrents of terror
To overthrow the monstrous predator.

The fact is that the degree of personal agitation created by detest for the stubborn habit is proportional to the degree of freedom from such ignoble lifestyle. The agitation has to grow the point where the victim is ready to move out of the comfort zone, ready to take a risk, ready to move from breakdown to breakthrough and ready to die or live for something more valuable than the stubborn habit.

Focusing on the consequences of the stubborn habits as well as the gains of victory will enhance the development of detest for them.

Practicing Delayed Gratification

We are familiar with such wise saying as *no pressure, no pleasure. No price, no prize. Pay now and play later.* This is consistent with the principle of delayed gratification which is based on the denial of immediate rewards or gain for the purpose of obtaining a greater reward.

Most people live on the zone of least resistance. They actually degenerate to the point of becoming hedonists (people governed by the pleasure principles). Stubborn habits are rooted in as well as motivated by hedonism. They are costly lifestyles which consume resources. Lack of delayed gratification created the thief and terrorist, the pedophile and plunderer, the idolater and adulterer.

However effective practice of delayed gratification enhances mastery of life, as well as success. Sigmund Freud, in his psychoanalytic theory of human development noted that there are three distinct stages namely: *Id, ego and superego.* The id is the emotional and infantile aspect which demands immediate gratification. It also operates on pleasure principle, while the ego is the rational aspect which mediates between the two extremes of id and superego. The ego is the real personality. It is based on reality principle.

As we can observe, the ego aspect of Freud's human personality plays a major role in dealing with self-control, discipline and consequently is invaluable in promoting delayed gratification.

Some relevant questions to raise when one is confronted with the temptation or thought of engaging in stubborn habits include the following assessment questions:

a. Is this action or behaviour most appropriate for me?
b. Am I initiating a noble action or reacting inappropriately to a negative stimulus?
c. Is this the appropriate time and place to respond to the stimulus?
d. What will be the short, mid and long term gains or advantages for my action?
e. Will my action add or subtract value from my life purpose?

Ability to raise these questions as well as answer them is a true test of the individual's ability to practice delayed gratification.

The potency of applying these questions can be observed in the event that when a victim of stubborn habit is able to raise them and experience a little delay in initiating the ignoble act, he gains great impetus to quench the consuming flame of stubborn habits. The wisdom of exercising a little delay in jumping into engaging in the stubborn habit can be expressed in this way:

> *If one can exercise mastery over engaging in a stubborn habit for one minute, then one can exercise mastery over one's appetite for an hour. The mastery can grow into a day's mastery. Of course, it can develop into one week, a month..... The growing courage to resist the allurement and seduction of one second repeated 63 times, three months, one year now becomes the repertoire of knowledge which becomes a new lifestyle and the joy of successful living*

Employing Mind Control Mechanisms

We are actually what we are in our minds. Weak or strong, sane or insane (mad), negative or positive, doubtful or faithful, selfish or generous, unrighteous or righteous, defeated or more than conquerors- all these reveal more of our mental states than any other aspects of our lives.[49]

It is important to remind the reader that human beings have a tripartite nature of body, soul (mind) and spirit. The mind is the middleman and the control system. The human brain is the physical expression of the human mind. A three pound weight consisting of 30 billion nerve cells, the brain also contains 300 billion glial cells. The existence of this super machine in the uppermost part of the human body is a major reason why mankind is the chief steward of the earth. The human brain is superlatively potent, almost inexhaustible in capacity, ingenuous in creativity and amazing in productivity. In comparison to human usage of the brain, we are all scratching the surface. We are all swimming in shallow waters. The testimonial of this fact is that the best of us has only employed just about 10% of our brain power. In fact the great German-born theoretical physicist postulated that the best of humans utilized only 5% of brain capacity.

The realization of this huge and immense capacity of the brain (mind) is the solid foundation for every human being to gain freedom from stubborn habits. We all can control our thoughts and therefore our

---

[49] Passy Amaraegbu (2005). Transforming Your Mind for Exploits. Charismatic Forum Publications; Owerri, Nigeria.

habits. A few of the mind control techniques are discussed here. These include,

- Meditation
- Alternative focusing

Meditation

Note that every habit or attitude begins at the realm of thought. However with the passage of time and regular practise, the habit becomes an automatic action. It is carried out thoughtlessly.

Therefore, organizing an effective onslaught against stubborn habits will begin from being thoughtful. This is why meditation is an invaluable method of overcoming stubborn habits. Meditation means deep thinking, reflection or analysis (breaking down) of thought.

There are some basic conditions which enhance meditation. These include: the location of a serene environment, determination of period, usage of writing and relevant materials. Also, the position the individual assumes can be beneficial to meditation. Assume a position which will enhance alertness such as sitting, standing, kneeling or even lying down.

Reading relevant inspirational literature adds immense value to meditation. The Holy Writ and other inspirational literature which highlight the principles of acquiring noble habits as well as warn against the consequences are usually of immense value during meditation.

During such meditation sessions, one can dig up the root cause of the stubborn habit, the motivation, the gains and losses and based on these, arrive at a quality decision on how to overcome it.

Eureka is the word attributed to the great Greek, mathematician Archimedes who discovered how to determine the purity of gold. According to a source, Archimedes made this discovery in a bathroom. He had wrestled with this problem for a long time without success before he finally found the solution. It was a product of a long session of meditation. Eureka literarily means "*I have found it.*"

I recall that some years back in my battle against lust, I had a meditative encounter which came in the form of a mental image. While ordinarily I thought that lust was an invincible power, during meditative prayer, I had a correct image of lust as an old, weak and rag-tag worn out victim. Like Archimedes, I rose up shouting "I have found the solution. I have found the solution" and I really did.

Alternative Focusing
Whatever captivates the mind enslaves the entire personality. Whatever we focus on becomes magnified. We become the products of our predominant thoughts and imaginations.

But we all, with unveiled face, beholding as in a mirror, the glory of the Lord, are being transformed into the same image from glory to glory, just as by the Spirit of the Lord.[50]

Instead of focusing on the thought of the stubborn habit, one deliberately chooses to concentrate on how to overcome it as well as acquire positive habit. Naturally, most human beings are pessimistic. We tend to dwell on the negative as well as magnify it. We tend to forget the good and beautiful but repeatedly remember and make reference to the negative, disappointment and lack.

The strategy of alternative focusing demands that we acknowledge the reality of the negative but choose to dwell on the positive. Like the wise saying goes, *I may not prevent a bird from flying or even hovering over my head but I can prevent it from perching on me.* This is akin to the principle of personal responsibility. Nobody can succeed in any endeavor without assuming personal responsibility.

Also engaging in alternative focusing involves the pursuit of purpose. In summary, the human mind is empowered to be creative, noble and productive. These positive qualities can be enhanced by feeding on inspirational literature as well as taking deliberate decisions to replace ignobility with nobility.

---

[50] 2Cor.3:18

Engaging in Systematic Desensitization

It is a form of Behaviour Modification technique which uses "hierarchical schedule of increasing anxiety- provoking situations involving the phobic stimulus repeatedly paired with a response that is physiologically incompatible with fear and anxiety"[51]

Systematic desensitization (SD) was developed by the South African-US psychiatrist, Joseph Wolpe (1915-1997). Every stubborn habit may not fit in directly as an anxiety provoking stimulus but SD is used here in the sense of employing the principle of developing a hierarchical order of dealing with stubborn habits.

It is obviously frustrating and overwhelmingly problematic to attempt to tackle any stubborn habit with one sledge hammer, or a cure for all therapy. Consequently, a step by step or stage by stage approach is more preferable. This is what is involved in SD. For instance, SD personal approach to tackle kleptomania may take this form.

a. Learn through discussion that money is available.
b. See the huge money in the company of others(without the owner).
c. See the huge sum of money in the company of the owner.
d. Touch the money in the company of the owner.
e. Touch the money in the company of others.

---

[51] (Andrew M. Colman (2006) Oxford Dictionary of Psychological; New York; Oxford University Press)

f. Think of stealing the money.
g. Plan to steal the money.
h. Steal the plan in secret.
i. Steal the money in the presence of others.
j. Steal the money in the presence of the owner.

Next, one determines the incompatible anxiety-provoking stimulus to pair with the stages of kleptomaniac response. The noxious stimulus can be a graduated electric shock. Consequently, at any stage or step, the kleptomaniac manifests a strong urge to engage in active stealing behaviour (1-10), the electric shock will be applied to him/her. The idea of pairing the impulsive stealing behaviour with a noxious or painful stimulus is to cause the extinction of the former. The kleptomaniac may be comfortable from stages 1-6 but at stage 7, he/she may become restless and goes into the action of stealing. The introduction of the electric shock will act as a deterrent of course. The result may not be automatic. The pairing of undesirable response or stubborn habit with the painful stimulus (electric shock) has to be carried out repeatedly until two targets are achieved:

a. The victim of stubborn habit (in this case, kleptomaniac) learns to associate every kleptomaniac behaviour with painful response (in this case delivery of electric shock).
b. The direct consequence of this is the weakening and eventual extinction of the stubborn habit.

Though this method or approach can be attempted by victims, it is best handled by professionals of behavioural science such as clinical psychologists and psychiatrists.

Summary

This chapter serves as a practical guide to breaking stubborn habits. It is only a guide. The stages may be reversed or reordered based on peculiar individual needs of people.

These practical steps by step strategies for breaking stubborn habits will be of immense help to everyone of us. First, seek to understand the root cause of stubborn habits and diligently take the prescribed steps to terminate them.

Personal Reflection

1. Do you think that this chapter is necessary and why?_____

_____

2. From a personal perspective, which approach would you prefer to use to understand this chapter-hierarchical inclusion or exclusion and why?_____

_____

3. Which of the five practical strategies is most significant to you and why?

_____

_____

4. What practical steps would you take to break your personal stubborn habit and why?

_____

_____

Chapter Twelve

QUESTIONS AND ANSWERS

The focus of this Chapter is to deal with some difficult issues which might not have been covered in the other Chapters.

Question 1: As an adolescent who found herself among peers who are sexually involved in pre-marital escapades, I resolved to be different. However, pressure mounted from both inside and outside me and in order to play safe, I began to indulge in masturbation. I feel terribly bad for my action but I am equally helpless in my condition. How can I break this evil habit of masturbation?

Answer 1: Note that your case is a classical example of stubborn habits with similar features, such as; being an ignoble attitude, repetitive, rooted in personal lust, operated in secrecy, etc.

The beginning point of gaining freedom from masturbation (and every stubborn habit) is to accept personal responsibility. In other words, eliminate all excuses. Stop the blame game. Next, identify an appropriate alternative practice to masturbation, such as: reading inspirational text, personal prayer time, visit a friend, engage in meditation, etc.

Endeavour to eliminate all the environmental conditions which promote and nurture masturbation, such as: loneliness, exposure to pornography, secrecy and hypocrisy.

The mind is the battle ground of all stubborn habits. Therefore, fill your mind with the relevant word of God as well as spend quality time studying other inspirational literatures. Understand that you are engaged in a protracted warfare against the kingdom of darkness. You may also benefit from engaging in both personal warfare as well as submitting yourself to qualified deliverance minister(s).

Question 2: How do I get out of the terrible deception I found myself in? For ten years now I have been married to an alcoholic. He hid this stubborn habit from me during the period of our courtship. It is only after the wedding that I discovered the mess I got myself into. What should I do – end the marriage or continue to suffer for my error?

Answer 2: First, I am glad that you have taken responsibility of the matter by accepting that you erred in judgement. Within the period of your courtship, you couldn't discern the character weakness of your future husband. Others will learn from your mistake. Rightly, courtship is a period of discovery of the real personality of each other. You discover the strength and weaknesses, likes and dislikes, temperaments, etc. Again courtship should be neither too short nor long. Except in peculiar situations, it should last for at least six months and carried out under the supervisory eye of experienced and elderly couples. Finally, a broken courtship is better than divorce.

Back to the answer of the question. Divorce may never solve the problem. Therefore, you may not consider it as an option.

Now that you have accepted personal responsibility for marrying an alcoholic, two of you have to work out the solution. Does he understand and accept that alcoholism is an ignoble habit? Get him to focus on the consequences of his misbehaviour as well as the gains of ending the habit.

Alcoholic Anonymous is a group of people with similar stubborn habits who meet regularly under the supervisory watch of some health or social welfare workers who assist them to break the ignoble habit of alcoholism. Your spouse can benefit from this group.

Of course, earnest praying and the practice of unconditional love will be of immense help to your spouse to recover.

Question 3: How do I break the habit of impulsive buying? I am afraid that no matter how much I earn in life, I may end up as bankrupt.

Answer 3: I do identify with your sense of frustration and fear. The habit of purchasing whatever catches your fancy and most often things that are of little or no use to one, is a terrible habit indeed.

One of the invaluable ways to terminate this ignoble habit is to be engaged in strict budgeting. Plan your expenditures before your money arrives and most importantly, follow your plan or budget.

Of course topmost in your budget plan are two crucial items, namely, give to God and self in that order. It is referred to as p*ay God first and self second.* This principle means that you should deliberately assign a definite percentage of your regular income to God and personal savings. You may begin with 10 percent each.

Besides the material blessings this principle bestows on your life, it teaches you invaluable success principles, such as: self-control, patience, altruism and fear of God. It helps you to become a prudent manager of your life.

Any victim of impulsive buying can also benefit from engaging in acquiring financial intelligence. This can be carried out formally, by enrolling in a financial institution as a student or in formally by studying relevant materials. One can be involved in both.

I had the privilege of helping a professional accountant deal with this challenge in his life. Therefore, submitting one's self to a financial mentor is a potent way of handling impulsive buying. A significant other like a prudent spouse or friend can also be of immense help in handling this matter.

Finally, the victim of impulsive spending should know that he needs to develop his character. It is an issue of integrity. The more matured one grows spiritually, the more one can exercise self-control over all forms of temptation.

Question 4: How do I get out of unforgiveness? In all sincerity I am deeply hurt. I am actually bleeding inside my heart. The reason is that my wife is involved in infidelity. I work hard to provide for all her needs yet she betrayed me twice. Her reason being that because she wanted to solve the problem of barrenness in our marriage she had to yield to the advice of her mother and mine to try and get pregnant outside our marriage. We have been married for 12years without a child. What should I do –forgive or divorce her?

Answer 4: Without mincing words, adultery is a terrible evil. It equals to betrayal and poisoning. Yet, adultery can be solved. From your question, one can see that your own case is that of conspiracy. Two important women in your life conspired with your beloved wife to betray you. It is a pity indeed.

However in their own understanding, they desired to help you solve the problem of childlessness. Their intention was good but their strategy was wrong – terribly wrong. As terrible as it is, some cultures encourage and use this method to solve the problem of barrenness in a marriage. It is fraught with a lot of problems.

Dear hurting husband of an adulterous wife, you have every right to be offended, angry and bitter. However, you must have a change of heart and mind so that you will prolong your health and life.

Truly, unforgiveness, bitterness and prolonged anger hurt the person who is harboring these negative emotions more than the one who caused them. These negative emotions are like chemical poisons. They damage the mind and soul just like chemical poisons damage the body. Please preserve your own life by deciding to let go of all the hurts or pains your wife caused you.

Whichever way you discovered her sin either by her open confession to you or that you discerned it yourself, make up your mind to let go. Truly, you may still feel terrible. You will still be feeling the emotional pain but first, decide to forgive her and your painful feeling will begin to disappear. In other words, your feelings respond to your decisions and not the converse.

Of course, it is necessary to hold discussions with your wife and your mentors or marriage sponsors. You will need to involve your spiritual leader(s) too. Divorce may never be the best option because love covers a multitude of sins.

Remarkably, both you and your wife will need to undergo some medical and laboratory examinations to ensure the safety of your health. Sexual relationship may be suspended temporarily, until these issues are sorted out.

Dear hurting husband, you will need a lot of patience and support. Allow your mentors and leaders to help you. If need be, your wife may go and stay with the family of your mentor for a while so that you will have time and space to meditate over the whole matter. Please ensure that this measure is a temporary one, if necessary.

Spiritual approaches, like: prayer, bible study and fasting will be of invaluable help during this trying period. Your wife will benefit from these spiritual exercises too.

She will need to make promises as well as eliminate conducive atmosphere that aided that problem. The two elderly women will be wisely and strongly advised to keep their hands off your home.

Contemporarily, there are many noble ways to end the problem of a childless marriage. These include: adoption, In Vitro Fertilization (IVF), hormonal treatments and their likes. You and spouse can explore these while praying and expecting a divine intervention.

Question 5: I am terribly afraid of driving. My husband feels frustrated with my inability to drive even after he bought me a brand new and beautiful SUV. The fear of driving was caused by an accident I had ten years ago while I was learning to drive. Another vehicle hit the driver's side while I was on the steering. Miraculously, I escaped unhurt but I cannot get that experience out of my mind.

Answer 5: Your case is typical of phobias. They are a group of anxiety disorders characterized by persistent fear. The consequent behaviours include: avoidance, looking for excuses and ways to disengage from the required behaviour. Examples of phobias include:

- Acrophobia – Fear of heights
- Agliophobia – Fear of pain
- Agraphobia – Fear of sexual abuse
- Amaxophobia – Fear of riding in a car
- Genophobia – Fear of sex
- Gelotophobia – fear of being laughed at

In a general sense, all mortals are afraid of one phenomenon or the other. This is one of the reasons psychologists say that mortals may be described as a group of Homosapiens with varying degrees of neurosis.

However, when the fear develops to an unreasonable degree whereby it hinders productivity like the case of phobia, it needs intervention. In the case of fear of driving a vehicle because of the fear of encountering accident, the victim needs help.

It is necessary to consult a psychologist or psychiatrist who will likely use the Behaviour Modification model of Systematic Desensitization to handle the phobia. Of course the victim can make some honest attempt to conquer her anxiety and fear by getting her husband or a trusted good driver to teach and model driving for her. The model will need to show much understanding as well as be patient while helping the victim.

Summary

I have used these five case studies alongside questions and answers as examples of stubborn habits that are common place. They are only representative but may be useful. I counsel that further questions can be directed to your psychologist, psychiatrist or counselor. I can also be contacted with this email address – drpassy@yahoo.com. Cheers.

Personal Reflection

1. What new insight have you gained from this Chapter?

   _____

   _____

   _____

   _____

2. Is there any principle or strategy you encounter in this chapter that you can apply to your life situation?

_____

_____

_____

_____

Epilogue

In concluding this discourse, I would like to draw inspiration from two great minds. First is the great German physicist, Albert Einstein who said that "the value of a man should be seen in what he gives and not in what he is able to receive."[52] The second is Martin Luther King, Jr, the great American nationalist, who said, that the "ultimate measure of a man is not where he stands in moments of comfort and convenience, but where he stands at times of challenge and controversy"[53].

These two men were addressing the issue of habit or attitude. The first was generosity versus stinginess and the other, courage versus fear. It is true that our habits or attitudes make or mar us.

Perhaps, it is only in eternity that humanity will be free from the throes and troubles, trials and temptations of stubborn habits. In fact, those who end up in hell will remain bound to stubborn habits while those in heaven will be bound to noble habits. The difference between success and failure, eternal bliss and doom, lies in the ability of every mortal to conquer stubborn habits. This book has generously

---

[52] https://www.brainyquotes.com *"The value of a man" (Accessessed Feb., 14 2017)*

[53] https://www.brainyquotes.com *"Ultimate measure of a man" (Accessed Feb., 14, 2017).*

offered us an immense opportunity to be equipped on how to obtain this advantage.

It would be a source of great joy to me if the reader not only possesses a copy but should study it as well as help others to do same. Of course, you may have to read this book more than once. We send it out with the prayer that this book will help you to experience personal growth and transformation.

ENDNOTES:

[1]Webster's Universal Dictionary & Thesaurus (Scotland, UK, Geddes & Grosset, 2005)

[2]Andrew M. Colman, *Oxford Dictionary of Psychology (Oxford University Press, New York:2006)*

[3]Charles Swindoll in Zig Ziglar, *Over The Top* (Spiritual Life Outreach, Inc. Port Harcourt, Nigeria:2003)

[4]William James, Brainy Quote.com.xplore Inc. (https://www.brainquote.com Accessed January 18, 2017)

[5]Passy Amaraegbu, *The Eagle Generation* (Canniff Trust Ltd., Owerri, Nigeria: 1997)

[6]Passy Amaraegbu (2005) *Transforming Your Mind for Exploits Egbeda*, Lagos: Nigeria. Change Business Services Ltd.

[7]Guardian Newspaper Limited, (Lagos; Nigeria: 5, August 2013:13)

[8]Romans 7:20,21

[9]America Psychiatric Association, 2000, *America Psychiatric Association,* 2000, DSM-IV text Revision, Washington, D.C.)

[10]Eph.4:27 (NIV)

[11]*1Cor. 15:33*

[12]https://www.google.com (Accessed 24/1/17)

[13]https://www.merriam-webeter.com/dictionary/recidivism   (Accessed 24/1/17)

[14]Gen. 19:26

[15]Heb. 11:24,25

[16]Jamesclear.com, *Behavioural Psychology*. "How long Does it Actually Take to Form a New Habit?" (Accessed February, 16,2017)

[17]Ibid Jamesclear.com

[18]Ibid Jamesclear.com

[19]Passy Amaraegbu, The Nigerian Prison Sector Reform Conference "Behaviour Modification As a Significant Remedy for Recidivism Among Nigerian Prisoners" (Abuja: June 2015).

[20]Leon Neyfakh Why Do So Many Ex-Cons End Up Back to Prison? www.slate.com/articles/news_and_politics_/crime/2015/10 (Accessed 25 January 2017).

[21]Centre of Disease Contral and Prevention. Costs of Intimate Partner Violence Against Women.

[22]*Bureau of Justice Statistics, Crime Data Brief. Intimate Partner Violence 1993) 2001, Feb 2003,*

[23]Carrison, Bonnie E. (1984) (Carrisoon, Bonnie E (1984), Children's Observations of Interpersonal Violence pp 147 -167) in A.R. Roberts (Eds) Battered women and their families (pp. 147-167) NY. Spinger, Straus MA (1992). Children as witnesses to mental violence: A risk factor for lifelong problems among Nationally representative sample of American men and women. Report of the Twenty-Third Ross Round Table. Columbus OH: Ross Laboratories.

[24]Stephen, R. Covey, The 7 Habits of Highly Effective People, UK London Simon &Schuster (1989)

[25]Mk. 5:25-34

[26]Ps. 61:3-4

[27]1John 1:9

[28]2Tim. 3:16

[29]1Pet. 2:1-2

[30]Heb. 5:12-14

[31]1Cor. 9:24-27

[32]Prov. 1:17

[33]Col. 3:16

[34]C.S. Lewis, The ScrewTApe Letters, San Francisco: HarperCollins edition (2001).

[35]James 5:16

[36]Isa. 58:6

[37]1Thess. 5:22

[38]Prov. 6:6-7

[39]1John3:9

[40]John 4:23,24

[41]1John 4:18

[42]Eph. 5:18

[43]Library timeless truths.org/music (Accessed January 24 2017)

[44]Galatians 6:14

[45]The Story Behind... When I survey The Wonderous Cross. www.plymonthbrethren.org/article (Accessed January 24, 2017)

[46]James 1:13-14 NLT

[47]Gal. 5:19-21 NLT

[48]Jn. 8:44 KJV

[49]Passy Amaraegbu (2005). Transforming Your Mind for Exploits. Charismatic Forum Publications; Owerri, Nigeria.

[50]2Cor.3:18

[51](Andrew M. Colman (2006) Oxford Dictionary of Psychological; New York; Oxford University Press)

[52]https://www.brainyquote.com Measure of A Man Quotes (Accessed February 14, 2017)

[53]https://www.brainyquote.com. The Value of A Man Quotes (Accessed February 14, 2017)

Bibliography

Amaraegbu, Passy. A. *The Eagle Generation.* Owerri: Canniff Trust Limited, 1997.

Amaraegbue, Passy. A. *Transforming Your Mind for Exploits*, Lagos: Change Business Services Limited, 2005.

Amaraegbu, Passy. A. *Behaviour Modification As a Significant Remedy for Recidivism Among Nigerian Prisoners*, The Nigerian Prison Sector Reform Conference, Abuja: 2015.

American Psychiatric Association, DSM-IV Text Revision, Washington DC, 2000.

Bonnie, Carrison. E. "Children's Observations of Interpersonal Violence" pp147-167) In A.R. Roberts (Eds) *Battered Women and their Famlilies.* (pp.147-167) NY. Spinger, Straus MA (1992). Children As Witnesses to Mental Violence: A Risk Factor for Lifelong Problems Among Nationally Representative Sample of American Men and Women. Report of the Twenty-Third Ross Round Table. Columbus Olt: Ros Laboratories.

Bureau of Justice Statistics, Crime Data Brief, "Intimate Partner Violence," (1993).

Centre of Disease Control and Prevention. "Costs of Intimate Partner Violence Against Women."

Colman, Andrew. M. *Oxford Dictionary of Psychology* New York: Oxford University Press. 2006.

Covey, Stephen. R. *The 7 Habits of Most Effective People*, London: Simon & Schuster 1989.

Guardian Newspaper Limited, Lagos (5 August 2013:13). https://www.google.com (Accessed 24/1/17).

https://www. Merriam-Webster.com/dictionary/ Recidivism (Accessed 24/1/17).

Jamesclear.com, *Behavioural Psychology.* "How Long Does it Actually Take to form a New Habit?"

James William, Brainy Quotes.com.xplore Inc. https://www.brainyquotes.com (Accessed January 18, 2017).

Leon Neyfakh. "Why Do So Many Ex-Cons End Up Back to Prison?"www.slate.com/articles/news and politics/crime/2015/10. (Accessed 25 January 2017).

Lewis, C.S. *The Screw Tape Letters*, San Francisco: HarperCollins Edition 2001.

Library timeless.org/music (Accessed January 24, 2017).

Swindoll, Charles in Zig Ziglar, *Over The Top.* Port Harcourt: Spiritual Life Outreach, Inc., 2003.

The story Behind...When I Survey The Wonderous Cross. www.plymonthbbrethren.org/article (Accessed January 4, 2017).

Webster's Universal Dictionary & The saurus, Scotland Geddless and Grosset, 2005.

https://www. BrainyQuotes.com. Measure of A Man Quotes (Accessed February, 14, 2017).

https://www.BrainQuotes .com. The Value of a Man Quotes (Accessed February 14th, 2017.

ABOUT THE BOOK

Habits are as essential to human life as air. This central role of human habits defines the crucial nature of this book on how to conquer stubborn habits. *Break That Stubborn Habit*, is written from a practical viewpoint so that the reader can realize his/her potentials to live as a champion and winner.

The book is the product of experience and expertise. As a professional psychologist as well as an internationally trained transformational leadership expert, the Author presents a work which is relevant, educative, enlightening as well as authoritative.

The book covers such essential topics like, *characteristics, portraits and promoters of stubborn habits.* It includes a chapter on *recidivism* and finally concentrates on the issue of *principles of victory over stubborn habits.* Very remarkably, every chapter of the book ends with a section on personal reflection.

This twelve chapters' title is a potent life-changing manuel, an inspirational dossier as well as a reliable reference document.

ABOUT THE AUTHOR

Passy Amaraegbu, psychologist and preacher is the author of over twenty titles including the popular *Victory Over Lust trilogy*. An alumnus of three Nigerian Universities, Amaraegbu holds a doctorate degree in Clinical Psychology. He writes from his wealth of experience as one who gains victory over stubborn habits, from his professional training as a Behavioural Scientist as well as an accumulated and reliable expertise gained over many years of matching theory with practice.

Furthermore, the Author holds a second doctorate degree from Bakke Graduate University Dallas, Texas in Transformational Leadership. He travels extensively as a conference speaker, transformational leadership expert, psychologist and preacher. Dr. Amaraegbu and his wife, pharmacist Chimezie celebrated the silver jubilee of their marriage in 2017.

The Amaraegbus' with their five children, live in Lagos, Nigeria.

www.ingramcontent.com/pod-product-compliance
Lightning Source LLC
Chambersburg PA
CBHW072254270326
41930CB00010B/2374